The Greek Gods

An Illustrated Introduction

Matthew Leigh Embleton

Copyright ©2024 Matthew Leigh Embleton. All rights reserved.

The Greek Gods

The Primordials 1
The Titans 2
The Olympians 3
Aether (The Bright Air of the Heavens) 4
Aion (Time, Ages, and Cycles of Time) 5
Ananke (Necessity, Compulsion, and Inevitability) 6
The Anemoi (The Winds) 7
Aphrodite (Love, Lust, Passion, and Procreation) 9
Apollo (The Renaissance Man of the Gods) 10
Ares (War, Courage, Bravery, and Destruction) 11
Artemis (The Chaste Huntress and Protector) 12
Asclepius (Health, Healing, and Medicine) 13
Asteria (The Starry One) 14
Astraeus (The Dusk) 15
Athena (Wisdom, Strategy, Battle, and Crafts) 16
Atlas (The Bearer of the Heavens) 17
Calliope (The Muse with the Beautiful Voice) 18
Chaos (The Void) 19
Chloris (Spring, Flowers, and New Growth) 20
Chronos (Time, Ages, and Cycles of Time) 21
Clio (Muse of History) 22
Coeus (Intelligence, Query, Axis of the Heavens) 23
Crius (Ruler of the Spring) 24
Cronus (Time and the Harvest) 25
Cybele (Great Mother of the Mountains) 26
Deimos (Fear and Dread) 27
Demeter (Agriculture, Fertility, and the Harvest) 28
Dione (Oracle of the Sea) 29
Dionysus (Wine, Fertility, and Festivity) 30
Eileithyia (Childbirth and Midwifery) 31
Enyo (War) 32
Eos (The Dawn) 33
Epione (Health, Healing, and the Soothing of Pain) 34
Erato (Muse of Love Poetry and Mime) 35
Erebus (The Darkness) 36
Eris (Strife and Discord) 37
Eros (Love and Desire) 38
Eurynome (Wide Ruler of the Pastures) 39
Euterpe (Muse of Music, the Giver of Delight) 40
Gaia (Mother Earth) 41
Hades (The Underworld and the Dead) 42
Harmonia (Harmony and Concord) 43
Hebe (Eternal Youth, and Forgiveness) 44
Hecate (Magic, Spells, the Moon, and Crossroads) 45
Helios (The Sun) 46
Hemera (The Day) 47
Hephaestus (Blacksmith of the Gods) 48
Hera (Queen of the Gods) 49
Hermes (The Divine Messenger) 50
The Hesperides (Nymphs of the Sunset) 51

- Hestia (The Sacred Fire) 52
- The Horae (The Hours and the Seasons) 53
- Hydros (The Primordial Waters) 54
- Hygieia (Health, Healing, and Hygiene) 55
- Hyperion (Heavenly Light) 56
- Hypnos (Sleep) 57
- Iapetus (Mortality and the Mortal Life Span) 58
- Iris (The Rainbow Messenger) 59
- The Keres (The Spirits of Death) 60
- Melpomene (Muse of Tragedy) 61
- Mnemosyne (Memory and Remembrance) 62
- The Moirai (The Three Fates) 63
- Momus (Mockery, Satire, and Criticism) 64
- Moros (Impending Doom) 65
- Morpheus (The Shaper of Dreams) 66
- Nemesis (Divine Retributive Justice) 67
- Nike (Victory) 68
- Nyx (The Night) 69
- Oceanus (The Earth-Encircling River) 70
- The Oneiroi (The Dream Spirits) 71
- Persephone (The Underworld and Spring Growth) 72
- Phanes (The Creator) 73
- Phobos (Fear) 74
- Phoebe (The Shining One) 75
- Physis (Nature and the Natural Order) 76
- Polyhymnia (Muse of Sacred Poetry and Hymns) 77
- Pontus (God of the Waters) 78
- Poseidon (God of the Sea) 79
- Prometheus (Forethought and Fire) 80
- Rhea (Queen of the Heavens) 81
- Selene (The Moon) 82
- Tartarus (The Darkest Depths) 83
- Terpsichore (Muse of Dance) 84
- Tethys (The Earth-Nourishing Waters) 85
- Thalassa (The Primordial Sea) 86
- Thalia (Muse of Comedy) 87
- Thanatos (Peaceful Death) 88
- Theia (The Wide-Shining One) 89
- Themis (Divine Order, Justice, and Custom) 90
- Thesis (Creation) 91
- Triton (God of the Depths of the Sea) 92
- Tyche (Goddess of Fortune and Luck) 93
- Urania (Muse of Astronomy) 94
- Uranus (God of the Sky) 95
- Zeus (King of the Gods) 96

Cover: The Parthenon
Source: AI Generated by the author

Acknowledgments

I have long been fascinated by languages and history, and I am very grateful to the special people in my life who have supported and encouraged me in my work. Thank you for believing in me. You know who you are.

Introduction

Who are the Greek gods?

The Greek gods are the key players in Greek mythology, an ancient collection of narratives that evolved over thousands of years to explain the origins of the forces of nature around us, their impact on our lives, the nature of humankind itself, what it means to be human, our relationship with the earth and the cosmos, and our sense of place within it.

How many gods are there in Greek mythology?

If we include all of the major gods, minor gods, spirits, demi-gods, mythical creatures, etc. from all of the different traditions across the ancient Greek world, we would be looking at about five hundred at least, maybe even a thousand, and if all of them were included in this book, holding it and leafing through it would be a Herculean task, so this is an illustrated introduction to about a hundred of them.

Why are there so many gods?

In all the corners of the ancient Greek world, there were local gods that protected and assisted people in many different aspects of their lives. Major gods even had local nicknames or epithets to emphasise the different characteristics that people resonated with. Greeks who travelled far and wide through migration and trade learned of gods in other regions and brought them home with them, for example the Phrygian goddess Cybele in Anatolia, Asia Minor (modern day Turkey). The Spartans saw Aphrodite as a warrior and called her Aphrodite Areia (Aphrodite the warlike). They could have worshipped Athena for the same reasons, but Athena was an Athenian goddess (The Spartans and the Athenians were enemies). Those with particular cunning would pray to the gods of their enemies to gain any advantage they could.

How do we know about these gods?

They are part of the history of Western literature from antiquity to the modern day, and from the Renaissance period and the revival of a classical education, they have inspired generations of storytellers, artists, authors, poets, and composers alike ever since.

The original Primordial gods are more amorphous (ἁ-, a- = without + μορφή, morphḗ = shape, form + -ous) and elemental in nature and represent spaces and realms, whereas the later gods over time became increasingly anthropomorphised (ἄνθρωπος, ánthrōpos = man, human + μορφή, morphḗ = form, shape), especially when depicted in art, paintings, sketches, engravings, etc.

Hesiod's Theogony

Hesiod's Theogony (the birth of the gods) is an epic poem which weaves together all the many stories and traditions from across the Greek world into a single poem of 1,022 lines. It is considered by many to be the standard source and reference point for Greek mythology and the family trees and domains of the gods. Interestingly, Hesiod states that a bronze anvil falling from heaven would fall for nine days before it reached the earth, and would then take another nine days to fall from the earth down to Tartarus. Hesiod's Anvil has been pondered over and discussed by philosophers and physicists alike ever since.

Homer's Iliad and Odyssey

Homer is considered to be one of the most revered and influential authors in history. His Iliad and Odyssey are two epic poems that deal with the Trojan War and the return of Odysseus to the island of Ithaca. The gods are frequently mentioned in both works as they choose to back different sides in the Trojan War and help or hinder Odysseus on his travels.

The Orphic Tradition

The Orphic tradition of beliefs originated in Thrace where the collected literature is ascribed to the mythical Thracian poet Orpheus (who according to legend descended into the Underworld and returned to tell the tale, something previously thought impossible). The body of Orphic literature includes the Orphic Hymns, the Argonautica, and the Derveni papyrus. A significant difference in the Orphic tradition is the concept of the Orphic Egg (the Cosmic-Egg or the World-Egg) out of which hatched the creator Phanes along with the primordial matter that he used to create the gods, the earth, the sea, and the sky.

Why are there so many different versions of the same stories?

There were at least five hundred years of oral tradition and storytelling all over the Greek world before the events and relationships between the gods started to be written down. There were always multiple versions of the myths steadily evolving, depending on where you were, and who was telling the tale. It was the author's choice which versions they used, and they could distinguish themselves by using the well known source material to tell their version, embellishing here, making a few changes there, putting their own stamp on it, hopefully saying something new and interesting or adding a deeper meaning somewhere.

If we only look at one source, we miss out. For example, it is not until Ovid's Metamorphoses in the first Century CE that we hear of Morpheus (one of my favourites) being named as the leader of the Oneiroi (the dream spirits). Other writers down the ages such as Aeschylus, Publius Vergilius Maro, Gaius Julius Hyginus, Ovid, and Nonnus of Panopolis all added their contribution to the tradition. In the 10th century the Byzantine encyclopaedia of the ancient Mediterranean world known as the Suda (or Souda) collected and preserved many ancient sources that have since been lost.

It's all quite complicated isnt it?

Tell me about it... But that's also what makes it so fascinating. It's such a broad and multi-layered subject. No one will ever have the last word on it. For every person who tells a story, there will be another person who knows an additional detail, twist, or version of it.

Do people still believe in these gods?

People absolutely still choose to believe in the Roman gods in many different ways, and for many different reasons, i.e. paganism, astrology, etc., as they symbolise and represent so many aspects of who we are: our aspirations and failings, strengths and weaknesses, and hopes and dreams.

The Greek Gods   *An Illustrated Introduction*

The Primordials

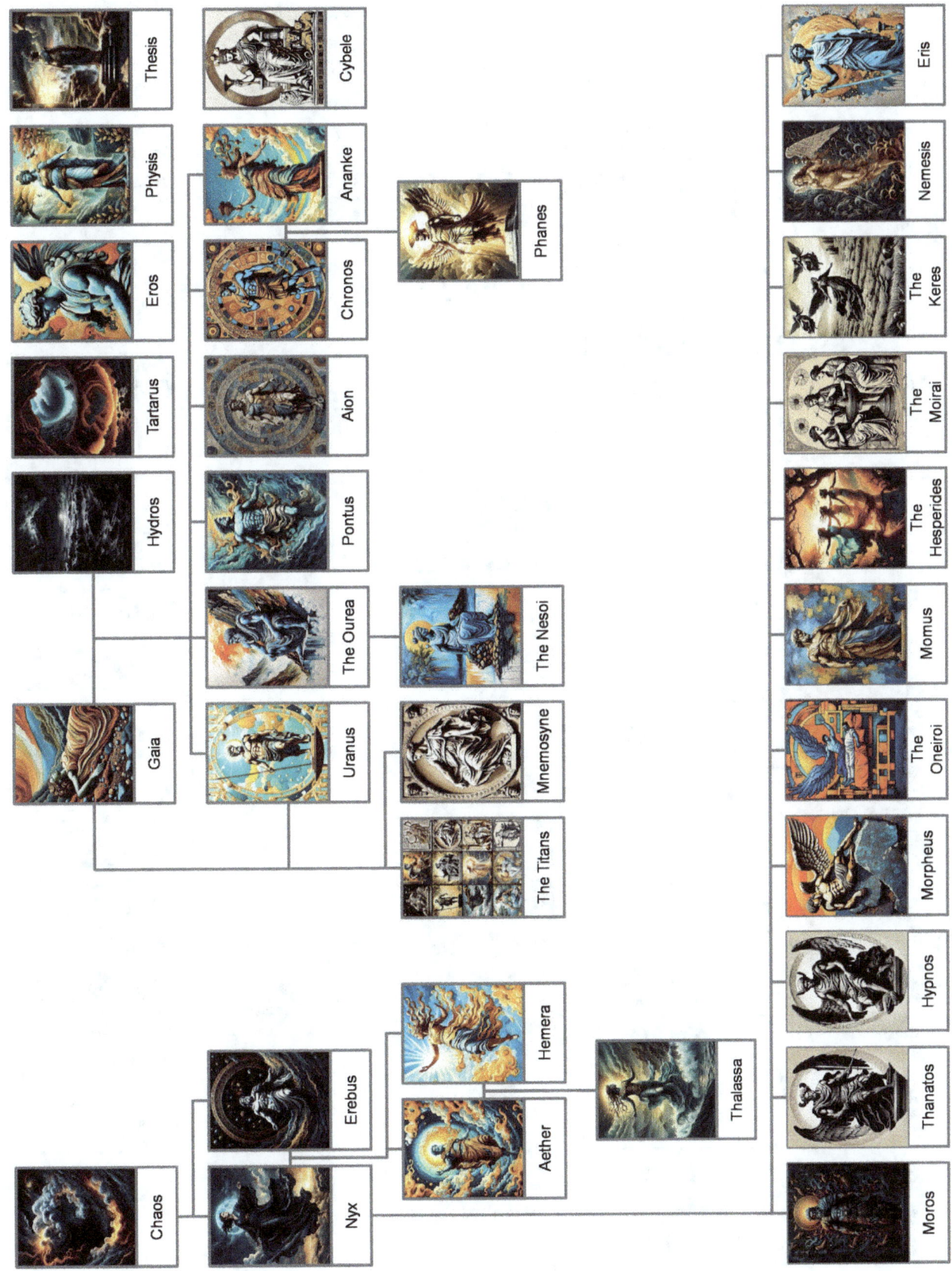

The Greek Gods — An Illustrated Introduction

The Titans

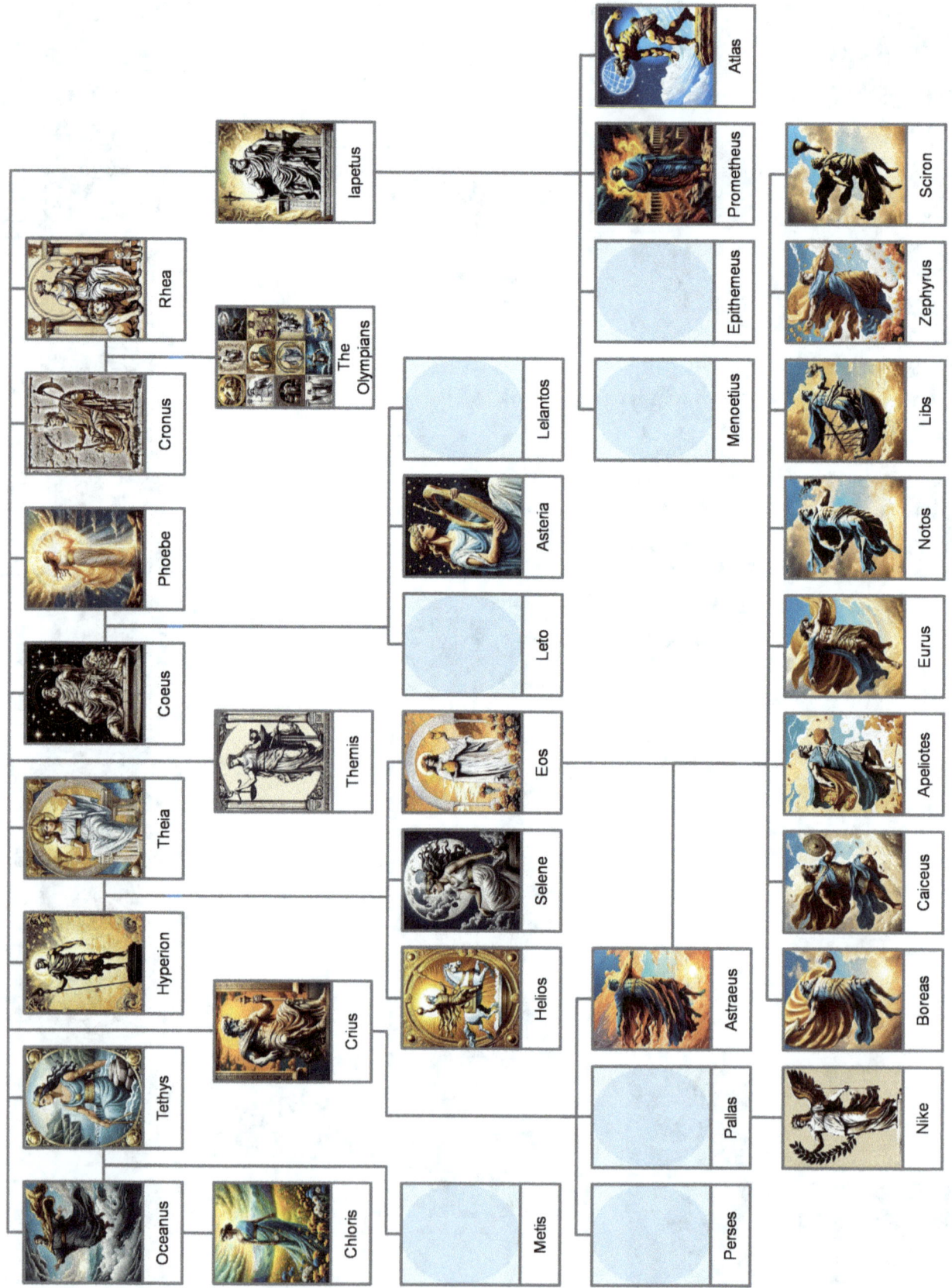

2

The Greek Gods — An Illustrated Introduction

The Olympians

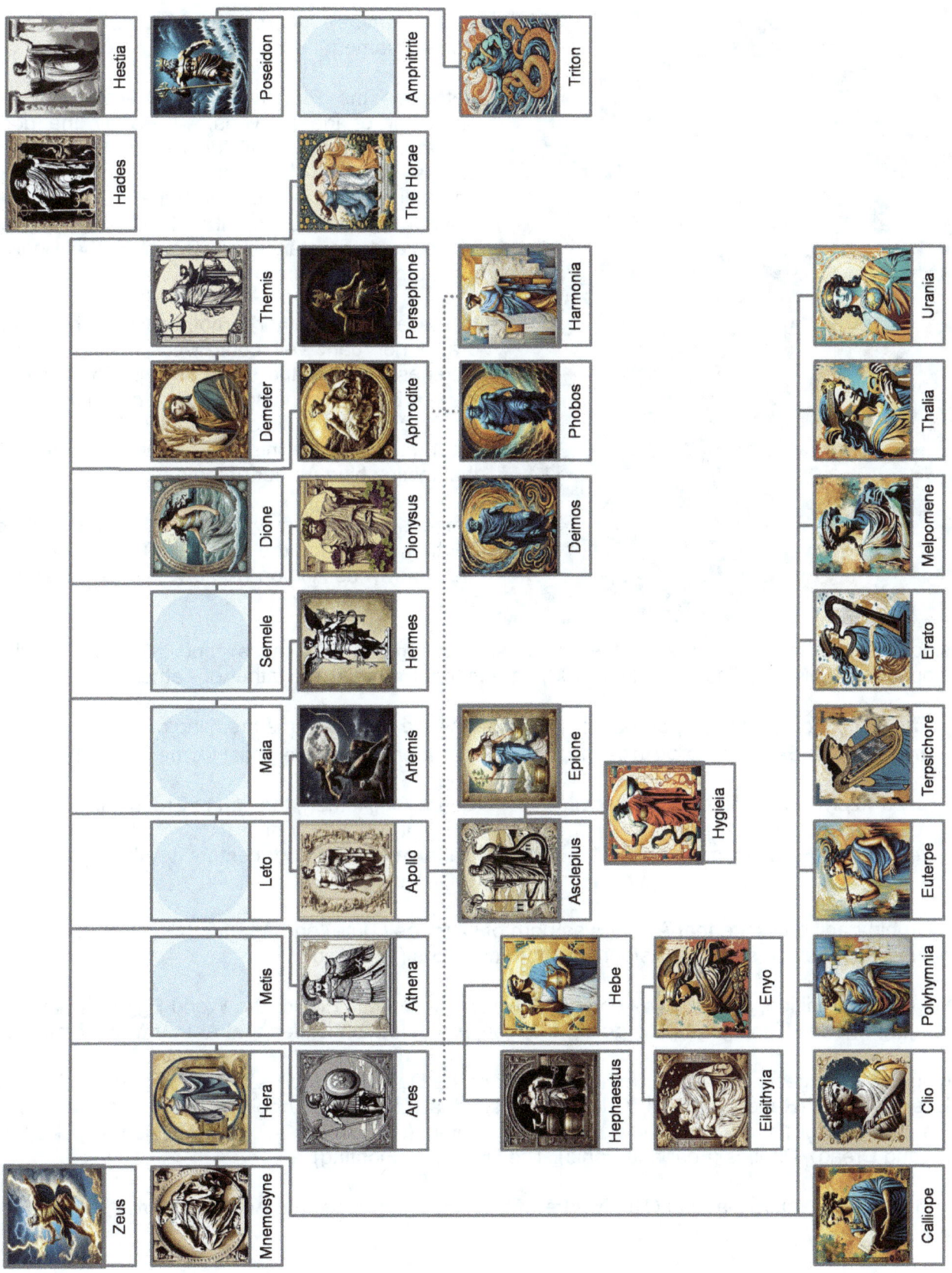

Aether (The Bright Air of the Heavens)

Greek Name(s): *Αιθηρ*, Aithêr, Aether
Roman Name(s): Æther

Aether is the Primordial personification of the bright air of the heavens, whose air the gods breathe. His thin mists fill the void above the dome of the sky and the transparent mists of the earthbound air. The mists of Aether also reach the highest mountain peaks, the clouds, the sun, the moon, and the stars. This is where the English word ether comes from.

In the evening Aether's mother Nyx (The Night) draws her dark veil composed of Erebus (The Darkness) across the sky, obscuring Aether from the earth and bringing about the night. In the morning Aether's sister and wife Hemera (The Day) disperses the mists of the night and reveals the shining blue Aether of the day.

Aether's female equivalent is Aethra or Aithre, another name for the goddess Theia. Aether is also known as Acmon (*Ακμων*, Akmôn), meaning zenith or untiring.

Hesiod's Theogony states that Aether was born of Erebus (Darkness) and Nyx (The Night). Aristophanes in his play The Birds (line 1189) agrees that Erebus is the father of Aether:

"πόλεμος αἴρεται, πόλεμος οὐ φατὸς *πρὸς ἐμὲ καὶ θεούς. ἀλλὰ φύλαττε πᾶς* *ἀέρα περινέφελον, ὃν ἔρεβος ἐτέκετο,* *μή σε λάθῃ θεῶν τις ταύτῃ περῶν:"*	"War, a terrible war is breaking out between us and the gods! Come, let each one guard Air [Aether], the son of Erebus, in which the clouds float. Take care no immortal enters it without your knowledge."

The Orphic traditions state that Aether was born of Chronos (Time) and Ananke (Necessity), whereas Hyginus in his preface says that Aether was born of Chaos (The Void).

In the Orphic tradition, Aether is the domain in which the Cosmic Egg or the World Egg was hatched, containing Phanes (Protogonus) the god of creation, which led to the idea that Aether was their father.

Hyginus also suggests that Aether fathered many of the Daimones (spirits): The Algea (Pains), Dolos (Trickery), Lyssa (Rage), Penthos (Grief), The Pseudea (Lies), The Logoi (Stories), Horcus (Oaths), Poine (Vengeance), The Amphilogiai (Disputes), Lethe (Forgetfulness), Aergia (Idleness), Deimos (Fear and Dread), Phobos (Fear and Panic), The Hysminai (Fighting)

Cicero in his *De Natura Deorum* (The Nature of the Gods) suggests that Aether fathered Uranus (The Sky).

Aion (Time, Ages, and Cycles of Time)

Greek Name(s): *Αἰών*, Αἰών, Aeon, Aion
Roman Name(s): Aion

Aion is a Primordial personification of time in the sense of ages, cycles of time (the year, the zodiac, etc.), perpetuity, and eternity.

This is where the English word aeon comes from.

Because of Aion's association with time, he has been identified and conflated with the gods Chronos and Cronus.

Chronos and Cronus have also both become identified and conflated with the Roman god Saturnus (Saturn) as a Father Time figure, particularly in the Renaissance period.

Aion is often depicted as a man (sometimes young, sometimes old) standing inside and turning a zodiac wheel decorated with zodiac signs representing the shifting constellations of stars and the cycles of time.

A serpent biting or swallowing its tail or hiding its tail underneath its body (an Ouroboros) is said to represent a cycle of time and also Aion himself.

As a god of cyclic ages, Aion appears as an icon in several of the mystery religions where the concepts of eternity and the afterlife appear, such as the Mysteries of Cybele, the Mysteries of Dionysus, Orphic Religion, and the Mysteries of Mithras.

In the Mysteries of Mithras, there also appears a lion-headed figure called a Leontocephalus (a lion-headed god), which is largely agreed by scholars to be a representation of time and seasonal change, and believed by some to be a version of Aion.

Aion also became a symbol and a guarantor of the perpetuity of Roman rule, appearing on coins issued by emperor Antoninus Pius.

In the Roman tradition, Aion's counterpart was Aeternitas (Eternity) or Anna Perenna (perpetual years), who was celebrated on the Ides of March (March 15th) in the old Roman Lunar Calendar when the year started in March.

Aion is also known as Porus (*Πορος*, Poros), meaning contrivance or passage.

The Orphic Fragments 54 and 57 state that Aion was born of Hydros (The Primordial Waters) and Gaia (Mother Earth), whereas Nonnus says that Aion emerged fully formed at the beginning of creation.

Ananke (Necessity, Compulsion, and Inevitability)

Greek Name(s): *Αναγκη*, Anankê, Ananke
Roman Name(s): Necessitas

Ananke is the Primordial personification of necessity, compulsion, and inevitability, both in terms of the beginning of creation, and in terms of the rotation of the heavens driving time and therefore driving destiny forward unstoppably.

In the Orphic tradition she emerged self-formed at the beginning of creation, initially envisaged as a serpentine figure with outstretched arms that encompassed the cosmos.

With her consort Chronos (Time), also in serpentine form, they coiled themselves around the Cosmic Egg or World Egg, causing it to split apart.

Out of this egg hatched Phanes (Protogonus) the god of creation, who created the earth, the sea, and the sky.

After their part in the act of creation, Chronos and Ananke then circled the cosmos, driving the rotation of the heavens and the eternal passage of time.

Ananke is sometimes depicted as holding a spindle, a symbol of the entwining and spinning of fate and destiny.

Plato, in his Republic, mentions the Moirai (the Fates) as the daughters of Necessity (Ananke), who are also depicted as spinning, measuring, and cutting the threads of fate.

In the ancient Greek tragedy Prometheus Bound attributed to Aeschylus, the Titan Prometheus accepts his fate and mentions Ananke (Necessity):

> *"I must bear my allotted doom as lightly as I can, knowing that the might of Anankê (Necessity) permits no resistance".*
>
> Aeschylus, Prometheus Bound 103 ff (c5th century BCE)

Ananke is also known as Adrastia (*Αδραστεια, Αδρηστεια*, Adrasteia, Adrêsteia) meaning inescapable and also Tecmor (*Τεκμωρ*, Tekmôr) meaning purpose, end, goal.

Orphic Fragment 54 suggests alternatively that Ananke was born of Hydros (The Primordial Waters) and Gaia (Mother Earth).

The Anemoi (The Winds)

The Greek Gods

Greek Name(s): Ἄνεμοι, Ánemoi, Anemoi
Roman Name(s): Venti

The Anemoi are the personifications of the winds based on where they come from, their points of origin on the compass, and the seasons they represent. The first four to be named were Boreas (*Βορέας*) the North Wind, Eurus (*Εὖρος*) the East or Southeast Wind, Notos (*Νότος*) the South Wind, and Zephyrus (*Ζέφυρος*) the West Wind.

The Tower of Winds in Athens, built around the first century BCE, is the only surviving horologium (clock tower) that remains from classical antiquity. On each of its eight sides is a relief sculpture of the winds as follows:

	NW	N	NE
Greek Name(s)	Skiron (*Σκίρων*)	Boreas (*Βορέας*)	Kaikias (*Καϊκιάς*)
Roman Name(s)	Caurus, Corus	Aquilo, Septentrio	Caecius
	W		E
Greek Name(s)	Zephyrus (*Ζέφυρος*)		Apeliotes (*Απελιώτες*)
Roman Name(s)	Favonius		Subsolanus
	SW	S	SE
Greek Name(s)	Libs (*Λιψ*)	Notos (*Νότος*)	Eurus (*Εὖρος*)
Roman Name(s)	Africus	Auster	Vulturnus

While the main four winds were the first to be named and remained fairly static, additional lesser winds were added, and some of their names changed over time.

Claudius Ptolemy (c100-c170 CE) was an Alexandrian mathematician, astronomer, astrologer, geographer, and music theorist. His work Geography or Geographical Guidance (*Γεωγραφικὴ Ὑφήγησις*, Geōgraphikḕ Hyphḗgēsis) is the basis for Ptolemy's World Map which is believed to have been produced by Agathodaemon of Alexandria in around the second century CE, based on the details given in Ptolemy's book.

In this map the winds are illustrated and named around the edges of the map, but instead of four (one every 90 degrees), or eight (one every 45 degrees), there are twelve of them (one every 30 degrees) which are as follows (clockwise from North):

• Septentrio or Aparctias • Aquilo or Boreas • Cecias or Apeliotes • Subsolanus • Vulturnus or Eurus • Euronotus • Auster or Notus • Libonotus or Euroauster • Africus or Libs • Favonius or Zephyrus • Caurus / Chorus or Iapix Sive Argestes • Circrus or Tresiias).

The Ptolemy map was the basis for the 1467 map of the world by Nicolaus Germanus. The Anemoi were included in several world maps up until the 16th century, such as those of Martin Waldseemuller (1507), Lorenz Fries (1522), Battista Agnese (1544), Giacomo Gastaldi (1548), Sebastian Munster (1550), and Abraham Ortelius (1564).

The Anemoi are agreed upon by many sources to have been born of Astraeus (The Dusk), and Eos (The Dawn). Astraeus was associated with the winds because of his sons, and also because it was believed that the winds were most active at dusk.

Aphrodite (Love, Lust, Passion, and Procreation)

Greek Name(s): *Αφροδιτη*, Aphroditê, Aphrodite
Roman Name(s): Venus

Aphrodite is the Olympian personification of love, divine beauty, lust, pleasure, passion, and procreation.

She is often depicted as divinely beautiful, representing an idealised form of femininity, and often accompanied with iconic symbols such as seashells, myrtles, roses, doves, sparrows, and swans.

The Astrological symbols for Aphrodite or Venus are believed to represent a copper hand mirror with a handle, or a necklace with a pendant.

In the 1750s the Swedish biologist Carl Linnaeus introduced the convention of using this symbol to represent the female sex.

According to Hesiod, Aphrodite was born out of the sea where Uranus's castrated genitals had been thrown by his son Cronus. In Homer's Iliad however she is the daughter of Zeus and Dione.

Plato in his Symposium argues that these two origins are those of two different entities, Aphrodite Urania (heavenly) as divine or spiritual love, and Aphrodite Pandemos (of all the people) as earthly love.

In the Peloponnese peninsula of Southern Greece, whose capital was Sparta, Aphrodite was worshipped as a warrior goddess with the epithet Areia (warlike) and often depicted bearing arms. For the Spartans, the warlike Aphrodite Areia would have been a symbolic alternative to Athena, who was the protector of their bitter rivals, the Athenians.

Aphrodite is believed to be Near Eastern in origin, similar to the Phoenician goddess Astarte, the Mesopotamian goddess Ishtar, the Etruscan goddess Turan (Apru), the Egyptian goddess Hathor or Isis, and even the Norse goddess Freyja.

The Roman equivalent Venus originally represented fertility and springtime, but from around the third century BCE, additional iconography in common with the Greek Aphrodite was adopted by the Romans.

As well as giving birth to many deities, Aphrodite had lovers who were mortal. She is the mother of the Trojan hero Aeneas in Greek mythology, and Roman tradition claimed Aeneas as the founder of Rome.

Venus then became venerated as Venus Genetrix, the mother of the entire Roman nation. Roman emperors claimed to be ultimately descended from her, and she took on the role of divine guardian.

Apollo (The Renaissance Man of the Gods)

Greek Name(s): *Απολλων*, Apollôn, Apollo
Roman Name(s): Apollo

Apollo is the Olympian god of archery, hunting, protection, healing, prophecy, light, truth, and the arts.

He is the personification of multiple ideals of masculinity and youthful masculine beauty, and something of a Renaissance Man among the gods.

The term Renaissance Man is used here with irony because:

1 - It refers to someone who is skilled in many disciplines in contrasting and complimentary fields (e.g. the sciences, the classics, and the arts).

2 - The Renaissance (rebirth) period of 15th century Europe saw a massive resurgence from east to west of classical culture, including preserved texts by Greek and Latin writers on the sciences, the arts, and classical mythology.

Apollo symbolises and embodies many qualities that were part of how the ancient Greeks saw themselves and what they aspired to, and perhaps this is why he is one of the more complex gods.

Apollo and his twin sister Artemis (born to Zeus and Leto) both symbolise archery, hunting, and the protection of the young. Apollo is credited with having invented archery, and such an invention is symbolic of brains over brawn or intelligence over brute force.

Even the Spartans, who famously saw the bow as a cowardly weapon, had to change their tactics and strategy after the Battle of Sphacteria in 425 BCE, during which they received a hail of Athenian arrows, to which they had no response. Apollo also symbolises military prowess in general. One of the astrological symbols for Apollo incorporates a bow and arrow.

Medicine and healing are associated with Apollo partly by association with his son Asclepius. Apollo has the power to deliver people from epidemics, but also the power to bring ill health and deadly plague with his arrows.

Apollo is also associated with prophecy and foresightedness. The oracles in the temples of Apollo were often consulted for guidance. He also symbolises the giving or bringing of light, the light of the sun, the light of truth and reason, and warding off the darkness of evil.

He presides over the arts, music, songs, dance, and poetry. Another astrological symbol for Apollo incorporates the outline of a lyre.

Ares (War, Courage, Bravery, and Destruction)

Greek Name(s): *Αρης*, Arês, Ares
Roman Name(s): Mars

Ares is the Olympian god of war who symbolises bravery and courage in war, and the physical valour necessary for success in battle.

The darker side to Ares however, is that he also symbolises bloodlust, brutality, and the destructive chaos of war, something phenomenally difficult to contain once unleashed.

As one of the less complicated gods, the ancient Greeks relationship with Ares was somewhat complex because of these two different sides.

His savagery and beastliness was the opposite of what the ancient Greeks aspired to.

In times of war however, the unleashing of such qualities alongside bravery and valour is perhaps a calculated risk, a tactical necessity, and a necessary evil when all else has failed.

The astrological symbols for Ares or Mars represent a shield and a spear. In the 1750s the Swedish biologist Carl Linnaeus introduced the convention of using this symbol to represent the male sex.

When Hephaestus discovered that his wife Aphrodite was having an affair with Ares, he trapped them both in a net and exposed them to the ridicule of the other gods, a narrative which symbolically checks Ares as capable of being outwitted.

Ares's affair with Aphrodite produced the twin personifications of fear Deimos & Phobos, and contrastingly the goddess Harmonia (Harmony) whom the Romans knew as Concordia.

As the Roman world expanded, Mars evolved from an agricultural protector to the protector of the Roman nation, becoming indistinguishable with Ares and ultimately the same god.

Hesiod's Theogony and Homer's Iliad, along with multiple other sources agree that Ares was born of Zeus and Hera.

Cities across Greece and Asia Minor held festivals to keep Ares as a protector, and to ask that his savagery and brutality be kept facing outwards towards any would-be enemies, rather than inwards towards self destruction.

"Under conditions of peace the warlike man attacks himself".

F.W. Nietzsche, Beyond Good and Evil (IV. 76.)

Artemis (The Chaste Huntress and Protector)

Greek Name(s): Αρτεμις, Artemis, Artemis
Roman Name(s): Diana

Artemis is the Olympian goddess of chastity, childbirth, midwifery, hunting, wild animals, the moon, the wilderness, and protector of young women.

She is a personification of multiple ideals of femininity and youthful feminine strength, skill, and chastity.

As a symbol of chastity, she is one of the three major virgin goddesses alongside Athena and Hestia.

The moment she was born from her mother Leto, she then assisted in the delivery of her twin brother Apollo, and she is therefore associated with childbirth and midwifery.

Artemis and her twin brother Apollo both symbolise archery, hunting, and the protection of the young.

Accompanied by her band of nymphs, the Pleiades (daughters of Pleione), Artemis roams the forests and the wilderness while hunting, sometimes at night, by the light of the moon. This led to her being associated with the moon, and with the goddess of the moon Selene (or Luna in the Roman tradition).

There are Roman Imperial copies of statues dedicated to Artemis-Selene (Roman: Diana-Luna) which combine the characteristics of the two goddesses into one, the originals of which date back to the 4th century BCE.

As well as a protector of the young, Artemis is capable of severely punishing those who offend her. She has the power to bring ill health and deadly plague with her arrows.

She is also seen as a protector of modesty, as exemplified in the cautionary tale of Actaeon, the young hunter in the woods who sees Artemis bathing naked. This angers Artemis greatly, and she punishes him by turning him into a deer, after which he is then devoured by his own hunting dogs who no longer recognise him as their master.

Artemis was one of the most widely venerated of the ancient Greek deities, with temples, altars, and shrines throughout ancient Greece. Her great temple at Ephesus was one of the Seven Wonders of the Ancient World.

Often depicted with a bow and a quiver of arrows, the astrological symbol for Diana (the Roman equivalent of Artemis) is the initial D fashioned as a bow and arrow.

Asclepius (Health, Healing, and Medicine)

Greek Name(s): Ἀσκληπιός, Asklēpiós, Asclepius, Aesculapius
Roman Name(s): Vejove, Vejovis

Asclepius is the Olympian god of health, healing, and medicine. He is the son of Apollo and the Triccaean princess Coronis.

In the Phoenician tradition, he was born from Apollo without a mother involved.

Some legends say that Coronis died in labour, and some say that Coronis was unfaithful to Apollo with a mortal named Ischys, and was killed by Artemis as punishment for betraying her brother Apollo.

Apollo learned of the betrayal from his raven Lycius, and later learned that Coronis was pregnant with their son, and when Coronis was laid out on the funeral pyre, Apollo cut the unborn child from her womb, which is where Asclepius received his name which means to cut open.

Asclepius was then raised by the centaur Chiron, who taught Asclepius the art of medicine. Asclepius became so proficient and skilled at medicine that he was able to bring the dead back to life.

This greatly angered Hades who presides over the Underworld and the dead, and so Hades asked his brother Zeus to punish Asclepius. Zeus destroyed Asclepius with a lightning bolt, after which he was placed among the stars as the constellation Ophiocus (The Serpent Holder or The Serpent Bearer) where he became a god.

Asclepius is depicted as a kindly bearded man holding a staff entwined with a snake. The Astrological symbol for Asclepius is known as the Staff of Asclepius which represents a staff entwined with a snake.

He is sometimes identified with Homer's Paean, the physician of the gods. The name Paean is also believed to be of Mycenaean Greek origin (*pa-ja-wo-ne*) and an alternative name for Apollo.

According to the 10th century Byzantine Greek Encyclopaedia known as the Suda or Souda (Fortress or Stronghold of knowledge), Asclepius and Epione produced the Asclepiades (children of Asclepius), five daughters and one son who represent different aspects of health, medicine, and healing:

• Hygieia (Health & Hygiene) • Aigle (Radiance) • Iaso (Healing) • Panacea (Cure-all) • Aceso (Curing) • Telesphorus (Convalescence).

Asteria (The Starry One)

Greek Name(s): Ἀστερία, Asteria, Asteria
Roman Name(s): Asteria

Asteria is the Titan goddess of the stars, night time divination, and goddess of the island of Delos.

Her name means of the stars or the starry one.

She is the daughter of Titans Coeus and Phoebe, and the sister of Leto.

She represents night time divination, such as astrology (by the stars), and oneiromancy (by dreams).

After the fall of the Titans, Zeus made many advances towards Asteria, chasing her across the sky in the form of an eagle.

She escaped him by transforming into a quail (ortux) and then flinging herself into the Aegean Sea.

Some legends say that in the Kingdom of the Sea, Poseidon then took up the chase.

She then avoided Poseidon by transforming into the wandering island of Asteria, the island which had fallen from heaven like a falling star, or Ortygia (the quail island).

After Zeus impregnated Asteria's sister Leto, Hera was furious and pursued Leto vengefully, ordering that no one should give her any shelter.

As a wandering island, Asteria disobeyed Hera's order, and offered shelter to her sister Leto, where she gave birth to twins Artemis and Apollo.

Apollo then fixed the island of Asteria in place where it became known as Delos, sacred to Apollo, and where Asteria became worshipped as their goddess.

Hera forgave Asteria for her disobedience out of respect for the way in which she had resisted Zeus's advances.

Asteria's association with divination is possibly inherited from the Delian goddess Brizo who delivered prophetic dreams.

Asteria's skill in astrology and prophetic dreams was passed on to her daughter Hecate (the goddess of magic).

Astraeus (The Dusk)

Greek Name(s): Ἀστραῖος, Astraios, Astraeus
Roman Name(s): Astraeus

Astraeus is the Titan god of the stars, the planets, astrology, and the dusk.

The name Astraeus is derived from the Greek word astḗr (ἀστήρ) meaning star.

As the father of the Anemoi (the Winds), Astraeus is also associated with the winds and the Dusk (the time of day when the winds increase).

According to Hesiod's Theogony (lines 375-380) Astraeus is a second generation Titan and the son of Crius and Eurybia.

"Κρίῳ δ' Εὐρυβίν τέκεν ἐν φιλότητι μιγεῖσα Ἀστραῖόν τε μέγαν Πάλλαντά τε δῖα θεάων Πέρσην θ', ὅς καί πᾶσι μετέπρεπεν ἰδμοσύνησιν".

"And Eurybia, bright goddess, was joined in love to Crius and bore great Astraeus, and Pallas, and Perses who also was eminent among all men in wisdom".

Hyginus on the other hand suggests that Astraeus is the son of Tartarus and Gaia, and one of the Gigantes (giants).

Servius the Grammarian, in his commentary on Virgil's Aeneid (1.132), wrote that Astraeus (as one of the giants) took up arms against the gods.

"Astraeus enim unus de Titanibus, qui contra deos arma sumpserunt, cum Aurora concubuit, unde nati sunt Venti secundum Hesiodum".

"For Astraeus, one of the Titans, who took up arms against the gods, slept with Aurora [Eos], from which the winds were born, according to Hesiod".

As well as the Anemoi, Astraeus and Eos (Aurora) the goddess of the dawn, also produced the stars, among them Phosphorous, the morning star or the planet Venus.

In the northern hemisphere, Venus is known as the light bringer, most brightly appearing in December due to the shorter days, signalling the rebirth of longer days as the winter wanes.

According to Nonnus in his epic poem Dionysiaca, Astraeus was an oracle who warned Demeter that her daughter Persephone would be ravished by a serpent and bear fruit from that union, which greatly upset Demeter.

Athena (Wisdom, Strategy, Battle, and Crafts)

Greek Name(s): *Αθηνη*, Athênê, Athena
Roman Name(s): Minerva

Athena is the Olympian goddess of wisdom who in times of war represents strategy, cunning, bravery on the battlefield, leading men into battle, and good generalship.

In times of peace Athena represents creativity, weaving, pottery, and handicraft in general.

She is commonly depicted wearing a shield and a war helmet, carrying a spear, and accompanied by her owl which represents wisdom.

Athena's father is Zeus, and her mother is Metis, a goddess of wisdom.

Metis was an advisor to Zeus and became his first wife. She was both a threat to him and indispensably helpful to him.

She had helped him to free his siblings from their father Cronus's stomach by giving him an emetic, causing him to vomit them all back out.

After Zeus had impregnated Metis, he immediately feared the consequences, especially when it was foretold that Metis would give birth to a daughter wiser than the mother, and then give birth to a son more powerful than the father who would overthrow him and become ruler of the cosmos in his place.

Zeus had overthrown his father Cronus, who had overthrown his father Uranus, and Zeus feared that he in turn would be overthrown by his own offspring. In an attempt to prevent Metis from giving birth, Zeus tricked Metis into turning herself into a fly, and then promptly swallowed her.

Inside Zeus, Metis crafted armour, a spear, and a shield for Athena and raised her inside Zeus's mind, where Metis remained and continued to be a source of Zeus's wisdom.

Eventually Athena used her spear and shield, banging them together to make a loud noise, giving Zeus an awful headache. When this headache became unbearable, Zeus had Hephaestus cut his head open.

Athena burst out of Zeus's head fully grown, fully clothed, and fully armed, and was then made the goddess of wisdom, warfare, and crafts.

Athena's Roman counterpart is Minerva, who appears in Etruscan mythology as Menrva, and comparatively in Egyptian mythology as Neith, Phoenician mythology as Anat, and Zoroastrian mythology as Anahita.

The Astrological symbol for Athena or Minerva is based on the head of a spear.

Atlas (The Bearer of the Heavens)

Greek Name(s): Ατλας, Atlas, Atlas
Roman Name(s): Atlas

Atlas is the Titan god of the heavens, and holder of the sky, also known as the bearer of the heavens.

His name comes from the ancient Greek tlênai (τλῆναι), meaning to suffer, to endure, or to bear.

Atlas has also been identified with the Etruscan god Aril, and the Egyptian god Shu, who is also depicted as holding up the sky.

He was a leader of the Titans in the war against Zeus and the Olympians.

After the defeat of the Titans, Atlas was condemned to stand at the western edge of the earth and hold the heavens aloft upon his shoulders.

He is also described as the guardian of the pillars which hold the earth and the sky.

He is often depicted as carrying the weight of the terrestrial globe (the world) on his shoulders instead of the celestial spheres, in which the stars and planets were embedded in an Aetherial transparent fifth element called quintessence.

Atlas is also described as the god who instructed mankind in the art of astronomy for navigation and to measure the seasons, and the god who turns the heavens on their axis causing the stars to revolve. This led him to being identified with Coeus who embodies the celestial axis around which the heavens revolve.

The Flemish geographer, cosmographer, and cartographer Gert de Kremer better known as Gerardus Mercator (Gerard the Merchant) chose to give the name Atlas to his binding of over 120 terrestrial maps.

His dedication of this binding was to Atlas the legendary King of Mauretania, the Latin name for the Maghreb where the Atlas Mountains lie, roughly corresponding with Morocco and Algeria today.

This led to the use of the term Atlas to describe bindings of terrestrial maps from the 16th century to the present day.

The Atlantic Ocean was also known as the Sea of Atlas because of the Atlas Mountains on the coast of Northwest Africa.

Atlas and Pleione produced the Pleiades (daughters of Pleione) the seven sister nymphs who are the companions of Artemis when she goes hunting.

Calliope (The Muse with the Beautiful Voice)

Greek Name(s): *Καλλιοπη*, *Καλλιοπεια*, Kalliopê, Kalliopeia, Calliope
Roman Name(s): Calliope

Calliope is the Olympian Muse of eloquence and epic poetry, and the eldest of the Nine Muses who dwell at either Mount Helicon or Mount Parnassus, the daughters of Zeus and Mnemosyne the goddess of memory.

The name Calliope means beautiful voiced, and both Hesiod and Ovid refer to her as the chief of all muses, being the wisest and most assertive among them. She is often depicted with a writing tablet in her hand, or a roll of paper, or a book, and sometimes a golden crown. The astrological symbol for Calliope represents a lyre, which is traditionally used to accompany poetry.

Ovid, in his Metamorphoses (5. 294-340), tells how she defeated the daughters of King Pierus of Thessaly, in a singing match. Then to punish them for their hubris and presumption in competing against her, she turned them into magpies.

Italian poet Dante Alighieri in his Divine Comedy references this story in Purgatorio, Canto 1 (7-12):

"Ma qui la morta poesì resurga,
o sante Muse, poi che vostro sono;

e qui Calïopè alquanto surga,
seguitando il mio canto con quel suono
di cui le Piche misere sentiro
lo colpo tal, che disperar perdono".

"But here, since I am yours, o holy Muses, may this poem rise again from Hell's dead realm;

and may Calliope rise somewhat here, accompanying my singing with that music whose power struck the poor Pierides so forcefully that they despaired of pardon".

She is believed to have been the muse and inspiration behind Homer's epic works the Iliad and the Odyssey. The Roman poet Virgil invokes her name for inspiration in the Aeneid (9.525).

"Vos, o Calliope, precor, aspirate canenti"

"You, O Calliope, I beseech you, aspire to the song"

The Roman poet Sextus Propertius in his Elegies (1.2 28-30) writes:

"Aoniam libens Calliopea lyram,
unica nec desit iucundis gratia uerbis,

omnia quaeque"

"Calliopeia, who loved Aonia's lyre, was unique and did not lack the pleasant grace of words,
everything of all."

Chaos (The Void)

Greek Name(s): Χαος, Χαεος, Khaos, Khaeos, Chaos
Roman Name(s): Chaos

Chaos is the Primordial personification of the gap or chasm out of which emerged the earth, the underworld below it, and the heavens above it.

She is the very first of the Primordials to have emerged at the beginning of creation.

Hesiod in his Theogony (116-118) writes:

"ἦ τοι μὲν πρώτιστα Χάος γένετ᾽, αὐτὰρ ἔπειτα Γαῖ᾽ εὐρύστερνος, πάντων ἕδος ἀσφαλὲς αἰεὶ ἀθανάτων, οἳ ἔχουσι κάρη νιφόεντος Ὀλύμπου,"

"In truth at first Chaos came to be,
but next wide-bosomed Earth, the ever-sure foundation of all
the deathless ones who hold the peaks of snowy Olympus"

Another name given for Chaos is Aêr (Αηρ), Aer, or literally Air. As a goddess of the air, Chaos is also the mother of all the birds, in the same way that Gaia (The Earth) is the mother of all land animals, and Thalassa (The Sea) is the mother of all fish.

Chaos later came to mean a disordered and confused mix of elements which existed in the Primordial universe jumbled up in a shapeless heap, which is where the modern English word chaos gets its meaning.

In some sources of the Orphic tradition, Chaos emerged from the Cosmic Egg or World Egg after it had been split open by Chronos (Time) & Ananke (Necessity). Some versions say that Phanes (Protogonus) also hatched at the same time, and then mated with Chaos, or that Chaos emerged from Hydros (The Primordial Waters).

Ovid in his Metamorphoses (1.5) writes:

"Ante mare et terras et quod tegit omnia caelum	"Before the sea and the lands and that which covers all the sky
unus erat toto naturae vultus in orbe,	there was only one face of nature in the world,
quem dixere chaos: rudis indigestaque moles	which to call chaos: raw and indigestible mass
nec quicquam nisi pondus iners congestaque eodem	and nothing but an inert weight accumulated in the same
non bene iunctarum discordia semina rerum".	a not well united discord are the seeds of things".

Chloris (Spring, Flowers, and New Growth)

Greek Name(s): Χλωρις, Khlôris, Chloris, Chloris
Roman Name(s): Flora

Chloris is the Olympian goddess of flowers and a nymph of the Islands of the Blessed, a realm of the Elysian Fields which is the final resting place of the souls of heroes and virtuous people.

Ovid's Fasti (194-198) reads as follows:

*"(dum loquitur, vernas emat ab ore rosas):
Chloris eram, quae Flora vocor: corrupta Latino
nominis est nostri littera Graeca sono.
Chloris eram, nymphe campi felicis, ubi audis
rem fortunatis ante fuisse viris,"*

"(While she spoke, her lips breathed out vernal roses):
I, called Flora now, was Chloris: the first letter in Greek
Of my name, became corrupted in the Latin language.
I was Chloris, a nymph of those happy fields,
Where, as youve heard, fortunate men once lived,"

The name Chloris is from the word Chlōrós (χλωρός) meaning greenish-yellow, pale green, pale, pallid or fresh. The astrological symbol for Chloris or Flora is a flower.

Chloris was abducted by Zephyrus (the West Wind), which is a parallel to the story of his brother Boreas (the North Wind) who abducted Orithyia. Chloris and Zephyrus produced a son called Carpus (Καρπός, Karpos) who is associated with fertility and springtime.

According to Ovid, Chloris was also thought to have been responsible for the transformations of Adonis, Attis, Crocus, Hyacinthus, and Narcissus into flowers.

She was also partially responsible for the creation of Ares, who Hera gave birth to in revenge for Zeus fathering Athena. Using a flower, Chloris made Hera pregnant with Ares, and Chloris was given a place in Rome as a reward.

Her Roman equivalent Flora is identified with the Oscan goddess of flowers Fluusa, which is evidence that her cult was widespread among the Italic peoples as well as the Greeks.

Her festival Floralia was held between the 28th April and 3rd May and symbolised the renewal of the cycle of life.

The festival began in 240 BCE, and in 238 BCE she was given a temple. For five days people would wear flowers and bright happy costumes, and farces and mimes were enacted.

Chronos (Time, Ages, and Cycles of Time)

Greek Name(s): Χρονος, Khronos, Chronos, Chronos
Roman Name(s): Saturnus, Saturn

Chronos is a Primordial personification of time in the sense of ages, cycles of time (the year, the zodiac, etc.), perpetuity, and eternity.

His name literally translates from Ancient Greek as time.

He is sometimes depicted with a sickle, representing the perpetual cycle of time and the harvesting of time and years.

Some accounts suggest that Chronos emerged from the union of the Primordial Waters (Hydros) and the Earth (Gaia).

Other accounts describe Chronos as having emerged fully formed at the dawn of creation with three heads (a man, a bull, and a lion) and the body of a serpent.

Together with his consort Ananke (Necessity), also in serpentine form, they coiled themselves around the Cosmic Egg or World Egg, causing it to split apart, out of which hatched Phanes (Protogonus) the god of creation, who created the earth, the sea, and the sky.

After their part in the act of creation, Chronos and Ananke then encircled the cosmos, driving the rotation of the heavens and the eternal passage of time.

Because of Chronos's association with time, he has been identified with and conflated with the God Aion, depicted standing inside and turning a zodiac wheel decorated with zodiac signs representing the shifting constellations of stars and the cycles of time.

Chronos (Χρονος) is most frequently conflated or identified with Cronus (Κρόνος) due to the similarity of their names.

Both of these names were identified with the Roman god Saturnus as a Father Time figure, particularly during the Renaissance.

In his work On Isis and Osiris (2.64), Plutarch states that the Greeks believed that Cronus was an allegorical name for Chronos, and that their Roman counterpart Saturnus (Saturn) is so called because he is filled (*saturatur*) with years.

Clio (Muse of History)

Greek Name(s): *Κλειω*, Kleiô, Clio
Roman Name(s): Clio

Clio is the Olympian Muse of history, and one of the nine Muses who dwell at either Mount Helicon or Mount Parnassus, the daughters of Zeus and Mnemosyne (the goddess of Memory).

Her name comes from the Greek root *κλέω* or *κλείω* meaning to recount, to make famous, or to celebrate.

She is sometimes referred to as the proclaimer, or the proclaimer, glorifier and celebrator of history, great deeds and accomplishments.

Clio is often depicted with a pen and parchment, a scroll, a book, a clepsydra (water clock), or a set of tablets with which she records her account of history.

The astrological symbol for Clio represents a quill writing on a book or tablet.

In 1593 Cesare Ripa published the first edition of his *Iconologia*, a hugely influential source book of emblems and allegories for orators, artists, and poets in the early Baroque period, in which he states:

"Pappresentaremo Clio donzella con una ghirlanda di lauro, che con la destra mano tenghi una tromba, & con la sinistra un libro che di fuora sia scritto TUCIDIDES".

"We will present Clio as a damsel with a laurel wreath, holding a trumpet in her right hand, and a book with the outside written Thucydides* in her left hand".

* Thucydides, a 5th-century BC Athenian historian and general

One of many conflicting accounts says that Clio had a son with Apollo called Hymenaeus, who became a god of marriage ceremonies, feasts, and song. Other accounts alternatively suggest her sisters Calliope, Terpsichore, and Urania as the mother instead.

Apollodorus tells that Clio derided Aphrodite for having an affair with the mortal Adonis. In revenge, Aphrodite made Clio fall in love with Pierus (Πίερος Píeros) of Magnesia, with whom she had a son Hyacinthus.

"Κλειὼ δὲ Πιέρου τοῦ Μάγνητος ἠράσθη κατὰ μῆνιν Ἀφροδίτης (ὠνείδισε γὰρ αὐτῇ τὸν τοῦ Ἀδώνιδος ἔρωτα), συνελθοῦσα δὲ ἐγέννησεν ἐξ αὐτοῦ παῖδα Ὑάκινθον,"

"Clio fell in love with Pierus, son of Magnes, in consequence of the wrath of Aphrodite, whom she had twitted with her love of Adonis; and having met him she bore him a son Hyacinth"

Coeus (Intelligence, Query, Axis of the Heavens)

Greek Name(s): *Κοιος, Πολος*, Koios, Polos, Coeus, Polus
Roman Name(s): Coeus, Polus

Coeus is the Titan god of Intelligence whose name translates as query or questioning. He is also described as the axis of the heavens, by which he is also known as Polus, as in the North Pole. In this role he is believed to be a god of heavenly oracles, just as his sister and wife Phoebe presided over the oracles of the axis of earth, which was Delphi, a role which was later taken over by Apollo.

Led by Cronus, Coeus and his brothers conspired against their father Uranus, laying an ambush for him as he descended to Gaia in order to lay with her. They waited at the four corners of the world and seized hold of Uranus, and held him down while Cronus, who waited in the centre, castrated Uranus with the stone sickle that Gaia had made especially, and then threw his severed genitals into the sea.

The brothers personified the great pillars holding heaven and earth apart. As Coeus personified the North Pole, Hyperion was the east, Iapetus was the west, and Crius was the south. After the Titans were overthrown by Zeus, Coeus and his brothers (except Oceanus) were imprisoned in Tartarus. Later Coeus was overcome with madness, broke free from his bonds, and attempted to escape from his imprisonment, but he was repelled by Cerberus, the multi-headed Hound of Hades (Hesiod suggests fifty heads, others suggest three). According to Pindar and Aeschylus, the Titans were eventually released from Tartarus because of Zeus's clemency.

Coeus is a relatively obscure figure in the mythology, but was important because of those descended from him. Together with Phoebe, they produced Leto who gave birth to Apollo and Artemis:

"φοίβη δ' αὖ Κοίου πολυήρατον ἦλθεν ἐς εὐνήν: κυσαμένη δὴ ἔπειτα θεὰ θεοῦ ἐν φιλότητι Λητὼ κυανόπεπλον ἐγείνατο,"

"Again, Phoebe came to the desired embrace of Coeus. Then the goddess through the love of the god conceived and brought forth dark-gowned Leto"

Coeus and Phoebe also produced Asteria who gave birth to Hecate:

"γείνατο δ' Ἀστερίην ἐυώνυμον, ἥν ποτε Πέρσης ἠγάγετ' ἐς μέγα δῶμα φίλην κεκλῆσθαι ἄκοιτιν. ἡ δ' ὑποκυσαμένη Ἑκάτην τέκε, τὴν περὶ πάντων Ζεὺς Κρονίδης τίμησε:"

"Also she [Phoebe] bore Asteria of happy name, whom Perses once led to his great house to be called his dear wife. And she conceived and bore Hecate whom Zeus the son of Cronos honoured above all."

Crius (Ruler of the Spring)

Greek Name(s): *Κριως, Κρειος*, Kriôs, Kreios, Crius
Roman Name(s): Crius

Crius is one of the Twelve Titans, and possibly the god of the spring, depending on how his name is translated from the ancient Greek.

One theory is that his name comes from *krios* meaning ram, referring to the constellation of Aries.

The springtime rising of Aries in the south was the first visible constellation in the sky at the beginning of the spring season in ancient Greece and the ancient Greek calendar.

Another theory is that Crius's name comes from kreion meaning ruler, which gives us less of a clue as to what he presided over or represented.

Led by Cronus, Crius and his brothers conspired against their father Uranus, laying an ambush for him as he descended to Gaia in order to lay with her.

They waited at the four corners of the world and seized hold of Uranus, and held him down while Cronus, who waited in the centre, castrated Uranus with the stone sickle that Gaia had made especially, and then threw his severed genitals into the sea.

The brothers personified the great pillars holding heaven and earth apart. As Coeus personified the North Pole, Hyperion was the east, Iapetus was the west, and Crius was the south.

After the Titans were overthrown by Zeus, Crius and his brothers (except Oceanus) were imprisoned in Tartarus. According to Pindar and Aeschylus, the Titans were eventually released from Tartarus because of Zeus's clemency.

Apart from his involvement in the castration of his father Uranus, Crius is mentioned less in mythological literature than other Titans.

Some scholars suggest that the addition of Crius into the ranks of the Titans is a means of making their number equal twelve, like the Twelve Olympians, where twelve is perhaps a significant and symbolic number.

While Crius may be something of a peripheral figure in the great scheme of things, his descendants are many and notable, including Astraeus, The Anemoi (Boreas, Notus, Eurus, and Zephyrus), Astraea, Phosphorus, the Stars, Perses, Hecate, Pallas, Zelus, Nike, Kratos, and Bia.

Another name for Crius is Megamedes (Μεγαμηδες, Megamêdes) translating as great lord.

Cronus (Time and the Harvest)

Greek Name(s): Κρονος, Kronos, Cronus
Roman Name(s): Saturnus, Saturn

Cronus is a Titan god of the harvest and of time, particularly when time is viewed as a destructive all-devouring force. He is often depicted with a scythe, or a sickle, or a harpe (a mythological sword or sickle) which he used to castrate his father Uranus.

Cronus conspired with his brothers against their father Uranus, laying an ambush for him as he descended to Gaia in order to lay with her. They waited at the four corners of the world and seized hold of Uranus, and held him down while Cronus, who waited in the centre, castrated Uranus with the stone sickle that Gaia had made especially, and then threw his severed genitals into the sea.

The sickle is also a symbol of the harvest. In Athens on the twelfth day of the Attic month of Hekatombaion, a festival called Kronia was held in honour of Cronus and the harvest.

Cronus feared being overthrown by his offspring, and so he swallowed each of them as they were born. When Rhea bore the sixth and final child Zeus, she spirited him away and hid him in Crete, tricking Cronus into swallowing a rock wrapped in swaddling bands instead. Zeus was assisted by Metis who gave Cronus an emetic, making him vomit back up the children he had swallowed. Zeus eventually overthrew his father Cronus and the Titans.

The astrological symbol for Cronus or Saturn evolved from the Greek κρ (khr or cr) with the cross being added in the 16th century. Cronus (Κρόνος) is most frequently conflated or identified with Chronos (Χρόνος) due to the similarity of their names and their association with time, however the former represents linear time (past, present, future), and the latter represents cycles of time (months, years, ages, generations).

Chronos means time, whereas Cronus is possibly from the ancient Greek word *kraínō* (κραίνω) meaning to rule or to command, perhaps because he was the ruler of the Titans. Both gods were combined and identified with the Roman god Saturnus (Saturn) as early as the 3rd century BCE, when writers like Andronicus referred to Jupiter (Zeus) as the son of Saturn.

Plutarch (On Isis and Osiris, 2.64) states that the Greeks believed Cronus was an allegorical name for Chronos, and the Roman counterpart Saturnus (Saturn) is so called because he is filled (*saturatur*) with years.

The Romans celebrated Saturn during the festival of Saturnalia which was held on the 17th December of the Julian Calendar. By the 1st century BCE the festivities had expanded from 1 day to 7 days. It was a time of feasting, role reversals, free speech, gift giving, and revelry. A sacrifice was made to Saturn at the Temple of Saturn in the Roman Forum. The planet Saturn and the day of the week Saturday (Saturni Dies, Saturn's Day) are named after him.

Cybele (Great Mother of the Mountains)

Greek Name(s): *Κυβηλη*, Kybêlê, Cybele
Roman Name(s): Magna Mater

Cybele is an ancient goddess of Phrygian origin (*Matar Kubileya* or *Kubeleya* = mother of the mountain) who was worshipped in the mountains of central and western Anatolia or Asia Minor as a mountain mother goddess, possibly the only known goddess in the region, or certainly the most important, and possibly a national deity.

The astrological symbol for Cybele represents a mountain.

She may have evolved from the traditional seated full figured fertility goddess found at Çatalhöyük in Anatolia dated to around the 6th millennium BCE.

The Greeks in Anatolia adopted and adapted her Phrygian cult and spread it to mainland Greece in around the 6th century BCE.

She became partly associated with the Earth goddess Gaia, and her Minoan equivalent Rhea, and the goddess of the harvest Demeter.

For some ancient Greek cults she remained something of a foreign and exotic mystery goddess associated with mountains, whose rites involved her traditionally arriving in a lion drawn chariot, accompanied by wild music and an ecstatic and disorderly following.

In Rome, Cybele became known as Magna Mater (Great Mother), and she was invoked as a key religious ally in the second war against Carthage from 218 to 201 BCE.

Roman mythographers interpreted Cybele as a Trojan goddess, since she had been worshipped in the broader Anatolian cultural sphere, of which Troy was a part.

Cybele became an ancestral goddess of the Roman people by way of the Trojan prince Aeneas who was the first true hero of Rome.

As Rome came to dominate the Mediterranean, Romanised forms of Cybele's cults spread throughout the Roman Empire.

As a protector of cities or city states, she was sometimes shown wearing a mural crown representing the walls of the city. Beyond this role however, there have been debates and disputes as to the overall meaning and morality of her cults, debates which have continued among scholars to this day.

Her images and iconography in funerary contexts, and the importance of the name Matar (mother) suggest that she is a mediator between the boundaries of the known and unknown, the civilised and the wild, the worlds of the living and the dead.

Deimos (Fear and Dread)

Greek Name(s): Δειμος, Deimos, Deimos
Roman Name(s): Metus, Formido

Deimos is an Olympian personification (daimon) of fear, translating literally as terror, specifically the dread and terror before battle, whereas his brother Phobos personifies fear and panic in the midst of battle.

The astrological symbol for Deimos is the lower case Greek letter Delta (δ, d).

Hesiod's Theogony (934-936) states:

"ῥινοτόρῳ Κυθέρεια Φόβον καὶ Δεῖμον ἔτικτε
δεινούς, οἵτ᾽ ἀνδρῶν πυκινὰς κλονέουσι φάλαγγας
ἐν πολέμῳ κρυόεντι σὺν Ἄρηι πτολιπόρθῳ,"

"Cytherea (Aphrodite), Fear (Phobos) and Panic (Deimos) bore, the shield-piercers
sufferers, who shake a phalanx of men thickly
in war with Ares, destroyer of towns,"

They are the sons of Ares (the god of War), who accompany their father into battle, driving his chariot and spreading fear in his wake, accompanied by Eris (the goddess of Discord). As sons of Aphrodite (the goddess of Love), they also represent the fear of loss.

In 1877 the American astronomer Asaph Hall discovered two satellites around the planet Mars, and they were appropriately named Deimos and Phobos. Deimos is the outer and the smaller of the two satellites of Mars.

In the publication Astronomische Nachrichten (Astronomy News), Volume 2, 1878, p.47 Hall writes:

> "Since there is but little need of names for these satellites, I have delayed in making a selection; but in order to avoid confusion, I have chosen the following names:
>
> Deimus for the outer satellite.
> Phobus for the inner satellite.
>
> These names were suggested by Mr. Madan, of Eton, England. They occur in Book XV of the Iliad, line 119, where Ares is preparing to descend to the Earth to avenge the death of his son".

The line which Hall refers to is here translated by R Lattimore:

> "So he [Ares] spoke, and ordered Deimos (Fear) and Phobos (Terror) to harness his horses, and himself got into his shining armour."

Demeter (Agriculture, Fertility, and the Harvest)

Greek Name(s): *Δημητηρ, Dêmêtêr*, Demeter
Roman Name(s): Ceres

Demeter is the Olympian goddess of agriculture, fertility, grains, the harvest, the earth, cultivated crops, sacred law, and the cycle of life and death. Her Roman name Ceres is where the English word cereal comes from.

The astrological symbols for Demeter or Ceres represent a sickle.

She is credited with the discovery of spelt wheat, the yoking of oxen, the ploughing, sowing, protection and nourishment of young seed, and the gift of agriculture, sustaining humankind with the earth's rich bounty. Before this gift of agriculture, it was believed that humankind subsisted on acorns, wandering without settlement or laws.

Demeter has the power to fertilise, multiply, and fructify plant and animal seed, and her laws and rites protect all the activities of the agricultural cycle.

With her daughter Persephone she was central to the Eleusinian Mysteries, a religious tradition that predated the Olympian pantheon, which may have had its roots in the Mycenaean period (c1400-1200 BCE). Initiates into the cult were promised a path to a blessed afterlife in the realm of Elysium.

Her cult titles include Sito (Σιτώ) She of the grain and Thesmophoros (θεσμός, thesmos = divine order, unwritten law + φόρος, phoros = bringer or bearer). The second of these was the subject of the secret female only festival called the Thesmophoria.

The Romans identified Demeter with Ceres, and the festival Cerealia was held in her honour from mid to late April, opening with a horse race in the Circus Maximus, whose starting point was opposite the Aventine Temple.

Demeter is assigned the zodiac constellation Virgo (the virgin) by Marcus Manilius in his 1st century work Astronomicon. In art, the constellation Virgo holds Spica, a sheaf of wheat in her hand.

Among Demeter's helper gods were • Vervactor, He who ploughs • Reparātor, He who prepares the earth • Imporcĭtor, He who ploughs with a wide furrow • Insitor, He who plants seeds • Obarātor, He who traces the first ploughing • Occātor, He who harrows • Serritor, He who digs • Subruncinator, He who weeds • Messor, He who reaps • Convector, He who carries the grain • Conditor, He who stores the grain • Promitor, He who distributes the grain.

Dione (Oracle of the Sea)

Greek Name(s): Διωνη, Diônê, Dione
Roman Name(s): Dione

Dione is an Olympian goddess associated with the sea and oracles.

She is identified by Homer as a consort of Zeus at the Oracle of Dodona.

This is the oldest of the oracles situated in Epirus in north-western Greece, which dates back as early as the 2nd millennium BCE according to Herodotus.

The name Dione comes from dîos (δῖος), meaning divine one often translated as goddess. It is a female equivalent of the name of the god Zeus (*Dyēus, Dios, Deus) and the Roman goddess Diana (Artemis).

There are around four or five different figures bearing the name Dione in Greek mythology. Some of these versions have elements that overlap or cross over, and some of them are different or contradictory.

According to Hesiod's Theogony (line 353), Dione is the thirteenth of the named few of the three-thousand Oceanids born of Oceanus and Tethys.

Apollodorus instead suggests that Dione was born of Uranus & Gaia. This is alluded to in sculptures such as the Great Altar of Pergamum, and the pediment of the Parthenon.

Hyginus agrees that Gaia is Dione's mother, but he suggests Uranus *or Aether* as the father.

Strabo in his work Geographica (Γεωγραφικά, Geōgraphiká) mentions Dione as being worshipped at a sacred grove near Lepreon on the west coast of the Peloponnesus, and being worshipped as a consort at the temples of Zeus.

Dione and Zeus are the parents of Aphrodite according to Homer, Euripides, and Apollodorus.

Hesiod however states that Aphrodite was born out of the sea foam that Uranus's castrated genitals were thrown into, hence aphrós (ἀφρός) sea-foam and Aphrodite meaning risen from the sea foam, however this etymology is now regarded as false by scholars.

Some sources suggest that Dione and Zeus are also the parents of Dionysus, but this is contradicted by other sources who claim Semele or Persephone as the mother, or Silenus as the foster father.

Dionysus (Wine, Fertility, and Festivity)

Greek Name(s): Διονυσος, Dionysos, Dionysus
Roman Name(s): Bacchus, Liber

Dionysus is the Olympian god of wine making, orchards, fruit, vegetation, fertility, festivity, insanity, ritual madness, religious ecstasy, and the theatre.

He is commonly depicted holding grapes and bearing a kantharos or wine cup. The astrological symbol for Dionysus or Bacchus represents grapes.

He is also sometimes depicted holding a thyrsus, a wand or staff of giant fennel, covered with ivy vines and leaves, sometimes topped with a pine cone, an artichoke, or fennel, a symbol of prosperity, fertility, and hedonism. The thrysus is a beneficent wand, but also a weapon to those who oppose his cult and the freedoms that he represents.

Those who partake in the rites and rituals of Dionysus are believed to become possessed and empowered by the god himself.

The Romans adopted Dionysus under the name Bacchus, a name of Greek origin, Bacchos (Βάκχος), meaning the frenzy that he is said to induce, known as *baccheia*. The Romans also identified him with their earlier god Liber or Liber Pater (the free father).

The wine, music, and ecstatic dance of Dionysus freed his followers from self-conscious fear and care. Wine was a religious focus, and could ease suffering, bring joy, and inspire divine madness.

Festivals of Dionysus included the performance of sacred dramas and enactments of his myths, which is believed to be behind the development of the tradition of western theatre, hence his association with the theatre.

His father is Zeus, but there are different accounts of who his mother is. Hesiod suggests Semele, Cicero suggests Selene or her forerunner Bendis, and others suggest Dione.

Dionysus was celebrated during the Roman festival of Liberalia, but the Roman state viewed the festival of Bacchanalia as subversive, because of the free mixing of classes and the transgressions of social and moral constraints, so much so that its celebration was made a capital offence, except for the state sponsored toned-down versions.

Academics previously interpreted Dionysus as a foreign god of Thracian origin who was only accepted into the Greek pantheon at a later date, since his myths describe him wandering abroad. More recent evidence however has shown that he was in fact one of the earliest gods attested in mainland Greek culture as far back as the Mycenaean period, dated to around 1300 BCE.

Eileithyia (Childbirth and Midwifery)

Greek Name(s): Ειλειθυια, Eileithyia, Ilithyia, Eileithyia
Roman Name(s): Lucina, Natio

Eileithyia is the Olympian goddess of childbirth, labour pains, and midwifery.

She has the power to further birth or protract the labour.

Her name means she who comes to aid or relieve from the Greek word *elêluthyia*, latinised as Ilithyia.

Her Roman counterpart was Lucina (light bringer) or Natio (birth).

When Alcmena was in labour with Heracles, Hera sent Eileithyia to stay the birth so that it would kill the mother and child.

However Alcmena's handmaiden Galinthias saw Eileithyia seated before the door with her arms and legs crossed, and cried out "a son is born!". Eileithyia leapt up in surprise, releasing her magical grip on the womb, allowing the child to be born. She was furious that she had been tricked by Galinthias, and turned her into a polecat.

Eileithyia is sometimes depicted as holding a torch, representing the burning pains of childbirth, and the bringing of children into the light.

In Homer's Iliad (XI, 269-271), Eileithyia is described as multiple goddesses:

"ὡς δ' ὅτ' ἂν ὠδίνουσαν ἔχῃ βέλος ὀξὺ γυναῖκα δριμύ, τό τε προϊεῖσι μογοστόκοι Εἰλείθυιαι Ἥρης θυγατέρες πικρὰς ὠδῖνας ἔχουσαι,"	"And even as when the sharp dart striketh a woman in travail, the piercing dart that the Eilithyiae, the goddesses of childbirth, send even the daughters of Hera that have in their keeping bitter pangs;"

Eileithyia has numerous shrines in many locations in Greece dating from Neolithic to Roman times. People would pray and leave offerings for fertility, a safe birth, and protection of their children, and also give thanks for a good birth.

Midwives had an essential role in ancient Greek society, with women of all classes participating in the profession, some whom would have been servants or slaves with only empirical or theoretical training in obstetrics or gynaecology. Those from higher social classes who were afforded a good education and training were referred to as *iatrenes* or doctors of womens diseases, who would have been respected as physicians.

Enyo (War)

Greek Name(s): *Ενυο, Ενυω*, Enyô, Enyo
Roman Name(s): Bellona, Bella

Enyo is the Olympian goddess of war. She is the female counterpart and close companion of the god Ares (Mars). The Romans knew her as Bellona.

Enyo was closely identified with Eris (Discordia) the goddess of strife. Homer identifies them both as the same goddess. She is said to delight in bloodshed and the destruction of towns. A statue of Enyo stood in the temple of Ares in Athens.

She is the daughter of Zeus and Hera, and with Ares (Mars) they produced Enyalios a minor god of war who appears mainly in Homer's Iliad.

"τοὺς δ' Ἕκτωρ ἐνόησε κατὰ στίχας, ὦρτο δ' ἐπ' αὐτοὺς κεκλήγων: ἅμα δὲ Τρώων εἵποντο φάλαγγες καρτεραί: ἦρχε δ' ἄρα σφιν Ἄρης καὶ πότνι' Ἐνυώ, ἣ μὲν ἔχουσα Κυδοιμὸν ἀναιδέα δηϊοτῆτος, Ἄρης δ' ἐν παλάμῃσι πελώριον ἔγχος ἐνώμα, φοίτα δ' ἄλλοτε μὲν πρόσθ' Ἕκτορος, ἄλλοτ' ὄπισθε."

"But Hector marked them across the ranks, and rushed upon them shouting aloud, and with him followed the strong battalions of the Trojans; and Ares led them and the queen Enyo, she bringing ruthless Din of War, while Ares wielded in his hands a monstrous spear,"

Eos (The Dawn)

Greek Name(s): *Hως, Êôs, Eos*
Roman Name(s): Aurora, Mater Matuta

Eos is the Titan goddess of the dawn who rises each morning and rides her two horse chariot announcing the arrival of her brother Helios (The Sun) and the beginning of the day. Her Roman counterpart is Aurora.

She is also the sister of Selene (The Moon). According to Hesiod she is the daughter of Hyperion (Heavenly Light), and Theia (Bright Shining). Homeric Hymn no. 31 to Helios gives another name for Theia: Euryphaessa, meaning wide shining (*eury* wide + *phaethô* shining).

Homer's Iliad mentions Eos's home as being at the edge of the river Oceanus:

"Ἠὼς μὲν κροκόπεπλος ἀπ' Ὠκεανοῖο ῥοάων ὄρνυθ', ἵν' ἀθανάτοισι φόως φέροι ἠδὲ βροτοῖσιν:"

"Now Dawn the saffron-robed arose from the streams of Oceanus to bring light to immortals and to mortal men,"

Eos has been given the epithet Rhododactylos meaning rosy-fingered or rosy-armed, a reference to the colour of the sky at dawn, and also Erigeneia meaning early-born. Homeric Hymn no. 31 to Helios reads:

"γῆμε γὰρ Εὐρυφάεσσαν ἀγακλειτὴν Ὑπερίων, *αὐτοκασιγνήτην, ἥ οἱ τέκε κάλλιμα τέκνα,* *Ἠῶ τε ῥοδόπηχυν ἐυπλόκαμόν τε Σελήνην* *Ἠέλιόν τ' ἀκάμαντ', ἐπιείκελον ἀθανάτοισιν,* *ὃς φαίνει θνητοῖσι καὶ ἀθανάτοισι θεοῖσιν"*	"For Hyperion wedded glorious Euryphaessa, his own sister, who bare him lovely children, rosy-armed Eos and rich-tressed Selene and tireless Helios who is like the deathless gods."

A goddess personifying something as fundamental and elemental to human daily life as the dawn can be traced back to the reconstructed Proto-Indo European name Hausos as far back as c.4500 BCE.

Traces of the name Hausos can also be found in the Roman Aurora, the Vedic Ushas, Lithuanian Aušrinė, Latvian Auseklis, and the Germanic Ēastre.

Eos together with her consort Astraeus produced the Anemoi (The Winds), and the stars, among them Phosphorous, the morning star or the planet Venus.

In the northern hemisphere, Venus is known as the light bringer, most brightly appearing in December due to the shorter days, signalling the rebirth of longer days as the winter wanes.

Epione (Health, Healing, and the Soothing of Pain)

Greek Name(s): *Ηπιονη, Επιονα*, Êpionê, Epiona, Epione
Roman Name(s): Epione

Epione is the Olympian goddess of health, healing, the soothing of pain, and the care needed for recovery. Her name comes from the ancient Greek word *epios* (ηπιος) translating literally as soothing.

Evidence suggests that Epione was a cult figure in Athens, Epidauros, Kos, and Pergamon. Asclepius and Epione both had marble statues in Argolis, where Asclepius was widely worshipped.

Pausanius in his Description of Greece mentions an image of Epione in Epidauros:

> *"ἐντὸς δὲ τοῦ ἄλσους ναός τέ ἐστιν Ἀρτέμιδος καὶ ἄγαλμα Ἠπιόνης καὶ Ἀφροδίτης ἱερὸν καὶ Θέμιδος"*
>
> "Within the grove are a temple of Artemis, an image of Epione, a sanctuary of Aphrodite and Themis,"

According to the 10th century Byzantine Greek Encyclopaedia known as the Suda or Souda (Fortress or Stronghold of knowledge), Epione and Asclepius produced the Asclepiades (children of Asclepius), five daughters and one son who represent different aspects of health, medicine, and healing:

Hygieia (Health & Hygiene), Aigle (Radiance), Iaso (Healing), Panacea (Cure-all), Aceso (Curing), and Telesphorus (Convalescence).

Erato (Muse of Love Poetry and Mime)

Greek Name(s): *Ερατω*, Eratô, Erato
Roman Name(s): Erato

Erato is the Olympian Muse of love poetry, and one of the nine Muses who dwell at either Mount Helicon or Mount Parnassus, the daughters of Zeus and Mnemosyne (the goddess of Memory). The name Erato comes from the ancient Greek word *eratos* meaning lovely, beloved, or desired.

As well as love poetry, Erato also represents mimesis (*μίμησις*, mīmēsis) the theatrical techniques of suggesting action, character, or emotion without words, using gesture, expression, and movement, which is where the English word mime comes from.

Since the Renaissance period she has been often depicted with a wreath of myrtle, roses, holding a lyre or small kithara, or a golden arrow representing the love she inspires. The astrological symbol for Erato represents a lyre, traditionally used to accompany poetry. In the Argonautica (3.1), Apollonius Rhodus invokes Erato at the beginning of the tale of the love of Jason and Medea:

"εἰ δ᾽ ἄγε νῦν, Ἐρατώ, παρά θ᾽ ἵστασο, καί μοι ἔνισπε, ἔνθεν ὅπως ἐς Ἰωλκὸν ἀνήγαγε κῶας Ἰήσων Μηδείης ὑπ᾽ ἔρωτι".	"Come, Erato, come lovely muse, stand by me and take up the tale. How did Medea's passion help Jason to bring back the fleece to Iolkos"

Strabo (c64 BCE – c24 CE), the geographer, philosopher, and historian, mentions Erato in his work Geographia. By quoting a poem called Rhadine by the poet Stesichorus (7th-6th century BCE), Strabo gives evidence that a place called Samus had existed, but has long since been torn down:

"καὶ ἡ Ῥαδίνη δὲ1 ἣν Στησίχορος ποιῆσαι δοκεῖ ἧς ἀρχή "ἄγε Μοῦσα λίγει᾽, ἄρξον ἀοιδᾶς, Ἐρατώ, νόμους Σαμίων περὶ παίδων ἐρατᾷ φθεγγομένα λύρᾳ""	"And further, the poem entitled Rhadine, of which Stesikhoros is reputed to be the author, which begins, Come, thou clear-voiced Muse, Erato, begin thy song, voicing to the tune of thy lovely lyre the strain of the children of Samos."

Diodorus Siculus in his Bibliotecha Historia suggests that Erato makes men worthy of love by her instruction:

"'Ερατὼ δ᾽ ἀπὸ τοῦ τοὺς παιδευθέντας ποθεινοὺς καὶ ἐπεράστους ἀποτελεῖν,"	"Erato, because [she] makes those who are instructed by her men who are desired and worthy to be loved,"

Erebus (The Darkness)

Greek Name(s): *Ερεβος*, Erebos, Erebus
Roman Name(s): Erebus, Scotus

Erebus is the Primordial personification of the darkness whose mists encircle the world and fill the deep hollows of the earth. In the evening Erebus's wife Nyx (The Night) draws her dark veil composed of Erebus's darkness across the sky, obscuring Aether (The Bright Heavens) from the earth and bringing about the night.

In the morning Erebus's daughter Hemera (The Day) disperses the mists of the night and reveals the shining blue Aether of the day. Erebus is also known as Skotos (Σκοτος, Scotus) also translating as darkness, and is sometimes also used as a synonym for the Underworld as a realm of darkness.

Hesiod suggests that Erebus was born of Chaos with no father. The Orphic tradition however lists Chronos (Time) & Ananke (Necessity) as the parents of Erebus.

Erebus and Nyx produced the Primordials Aether and Hemera (The Day). Hyginus and Cicero also suggest that they produced Eros, but Hesiod states that Eros emerged fully formed at creation. Erebus & Nyx also fathered a large number of Daimones (spirits, personifications):

• Apate (Fraus) • Deimos (Metus) • Dolos (Dolus) • Eleos (Misericordia) • Epaphos • Epiphron • Eris (Discordia) • Eros (Amor) • Euphrosyne • Geras (Senectus) • The Hesperides • Hybris (Petulantia) • Hypnos (Somnus) • Ker (Letum) • The Keres (Tenebrae) • The Moirai (Parcae) • Momos (Querella) • Moros (Fatum) • Nemesis (Invidentia) • Oizys (Miseria) • The Oneiroi (Somnia) • Philotes (Amicitia) • Ponos (Labor) • Porphyrion • Sophrosyne (Continentia) • Styx • Thanatos (Mors)

Eris (Strife and Discord)

Greek Name(s): *Ερις*, Eris, Eris
Roman Name(s): Discordia

Eris is the Primordial personification of strife, discord, contention, and rivalry.

Her name translates literally as strife, and her Roman equivalent is Discordia (literally discord).

In the Homeric tradition, she is portrayed as the spirit (daimona) of the strife and discord of war.

She accompanies Ares on the battlefield, delighting in the havoc and human bloodshed created, long after all others have left.

This has led to her being closely associated with the goddess of war Enyo, whom the Romans knew as Bellona.

In Hesiod's Theogony (226-232) Eris is described as the mother of a variety of allegorical beings representing the causes of humankind's misfortune:

Labour, Forgetfulness, Starvation, Pains, Fighting, Battle, Manslaughter, Quarrels, Lies, Stories, Disputes, Anarchy, and the breaking of Oaths.

In Hesiod's Works and Days (11-24) he argues that there are two kinds of Strife, the first representing war, the second representing the discord and strife associated with man's jealousy and competition with his neighbour.

ἥτε καὶ ἀπάλαμόν περ ὁμῶς ἐπὶ ἔργον ἔγειρεν.	She stirs up even the shiftless to toil;
εἰς ἕτερον γάρ τίς τε ἰδὼν ἔργοιο χατίζει	for a man grows eager to work when he considers his neighbor,
πλούσιον, ὃς σπεύδει μὲν ἀρώμεναι ἠδὲ φυτεύειν	a rich man who hastens to plough and plant and put his house in good order;
οἶκόν τ' εὖ θέσθαι: ζηλοῖ δέ τε γείτονα γείτων	and neighbor vies with his neighbor as he hurries after wealth.
εἰς ἄφενος σπεύδοντ': ἀγαθὴ δ' Ἔρις ἥδε βροτοῖσιν.	This Strife is wholesome for men.
καὶ κεραμεὺς κεραμεῖ κοτέει καὶ τέκτονι τέκτων,	And potter is angry with potter, and craftsman with craftsman,
καὶ πτωχὸς πτωχῷ φθονέει καὶ ἀοιδὸς ἀοιδῷ.	and beggar is jealous of beggar, and minstrel of minstrel.

Eros (Love and Desire)

Greek Name(s): *Ἔρος*, Eros, Eros
Roman Name(s): Cupid, Amor

Eros is the Primordial personification of Love and Desire. His roman equivalent is Cupid. He is depicted as either a young man or a boy with a bow and arrows or a flaming torch, which he uses to make gods and mortals fall in love. According to Hesiod's Theogony, Eros was the fourth of the Primordials to come into existence, after Chaos, Gaia (Earth), and Tartarus. He is said to have spurred on the procreation of the gods to bring about creation. In the Orphic tradition however, he was born from a cosmic egg laid by Nyx in the realms of Erebus:

Aristophanes in his comedy The Birds writes:

"τίκτει πρώτιστον ὑπηνέμιον Νὺξ ἡ μελανόπτερος ᾠόν,	"Firstly, blackwinged Night laid a germless egg in the bosom of the infinite deeps of Erebus,
ἐξ οὗ περιτελλομέναις ὥραις ἔβλαστεν Ἔρως ὁ ποθεινός,	and from this, after the revolution of long ages, sprang the graceful Eros
στίλβων νῶτον πτερύγοιν χρυσαῖν, εἰκὼς ἀνεμώκεσι δίναις.	with his glittering golden wings, swift as the whirlwinds of the tempest.
οὗτος δὲ Χάει πτερόεντι μιγεὶς νυχίῳ κατὰ Τάρταρον εὐρὺν	He mated in deep Tartarus with dark Chaos, winged like himself,
ἐνεόττευσεν γένος ἡμέτερον, καὶ πρῶτον ἀνήγαγεν ἐς φῶς.	and thus hatched forth our race, which was the first to see the light.
πρότερον δ' οὐκ ἦν γένος ἀθανάτων, πρὶν Ἔρως ξυνέμειξεν ἅπαντα:"	before there was no race of immortals, before Eros mingled everything:"

Eurynome (Wide Ruler of the Pastures)

Greek Name(s): *Εὐρυνόμη*, Eurynomê, Eurynome
Roman Name(s): Eurynome

There are several figures in Greek mythology with the name Eurynome. The name either means she who rules widely, from *eurys* (wide) + *nomos* (ruling), or she of the wide pastures, *eurys* (wide) + *nomia* (pasture).

Eurynome was the first Titan queen of the heavens who ruled from Olympus beside her husband Ophion. They were overthrown by Cronos and Rhea and cast either into Oceanus, the river that encircles the earth, or Tartarus, the lower realm of the Underworld.

Eurynome is also one of the three-thousand Oceanids born of Oceanus and Tethys. She is the goddess of water-meadows and pasturelands, and the third bride of Zeus. Together they produced the Charites (The Graces), whom the Romans knew as Gratiae (the goddesses of grace and beauty).

Eurynome is also one of the six daughters of the Greek hero Cadmus and the goddess Harmonia. Her sisters were Ino, Aguae, Semele, Kleantho, and Eurydike.

Eurynome came to the aid of the young god Hephaestus when he was thrown out of Olympus by Hera. In Homer's Iliad, he describes how Eurynome and Thetis saved him:

*"τότ᾽ ἂν πάθον ἄλγεα θυμῷ,
εἰ μή μ᾽ Εὐρυνόμη τε Θέτις θ᾽ ὑπεδέξατο κόλπῳ
Εὐρυνόμη θυγάτηρ ἀψορρόου Ὠκεανοῖο.*

τῇσι παρ᾽ εἰνάετες χάλκευον δαίδαλα πολλά,

*πόρπας τε γναμπτάς θ᾽ ἕλικας κάλυκάς τε καὶ ὅρμους
ἐν σπῆϊ γλαφυρῷ: περὶ δὲ ῥόος Ὠκεανοῖο*

*ἀφρῷ μορμύρων ῥέεν ἄσπετος: οὐδέ τις ἄλλος
ᾔδεεν οὔτε θεῶν οὔτε θνητῶν ἀνθρώπων,
ἀλλὰ Θέτις τε καὶ Εὐρυνόμη ἴσαν, αἵ μ᾽ ἐσάωσαν."*

"Then had I suffered woes in heart,
had not Eurynome and Thetis received me into their bosom
Eurynome, daughter of backward-flowing Oceanus.
With them then for nine years space I forged much cunning handiwork,
brooches, and spiral arm-bands, and rosettes and necklaces,
within their hollow cave; and round about me flowed, murmuring with foam, the stream of Oceanus,
a flood unspeakable. Neither did any other know thereof,
either of gods or of mortal men,
but Thetis knew and Eurynome, even they that saved me."

Euterpe (Muse of Music, the Giver of Delight)

Greek Name(s): *Ευτερπη*, Euterpê, Euterpe
Roman Name(s): Euterpe

Euterpe is the Olympian Muse of music, and one of the nine Muses who dwell at either Mount Helicon or Mount Parnassus, the daughters of Zeus and Mnemosyne (the goddess of Memory).

Her name comes from the ancient Greek *eu* and *terpô*, meaning giver of much delight, an epithet given for her by many of the ancient poets.

She originally presided over lyric poetry, but over time she came to represent music, song, and dance.

Euterpe's instrument is the aulos, a kind of double flute with a reed sound similar to that of the bagpipes, or the Northumbrian smallpipe.

She is credited with having invented the aulos and also other wind instruments.

The astrological symbol for Euterpe represents the two pipes of an aulos held together with a strap.

The difference between the music of the aulos and the lyre is symbolic in ancient Greece.

The lyre or the kithara also associated with Apollo represents reason and order, whereas the aulos associated with Dionysus represents freedom, madness, and insanity.

The aulos was thrown away by Athena, because playing it caused her cheeks to puff, which spoiled her beauty.

It was then picked up by a satyr called Marsyas who challenged Apollo to a musical contest, where the winner would be able to do whatever he wanted to the loser.

Apollo and his lyre beat Marsyas and his aulos, and Apollo celebrated his victory over Marsyas by stringing him up from a tree and flaying him alive.

Marsyas's blood and the tears of the nine Muses formed the river Marsyas in Asia Minor.

The tale is a warning against the sin of hubris, i.e. arrogance or pride before the gods.

Euterpe's role, alongside her sisters, was to entertain the gods on Mount Olympus.

She inspired the development of liberal and fine arts in Ancient Greece, serving as an inspiration to poets, dramatists, and authors such as Homer.

Gaia (Mother Earth)

Greek Name(s): Γαια, Γαιη, Γη, Gaia, Gaiê, Gê, Gaea, Gaia
Roman Name(s): Tellus, Tellus Mater, Terra, Terra Mater

Gaia is the Primordial personification of the earth, sometimes referred to as Mother Earth or Mother of all Creation. She is depicted as a voluptuous woman rising out of the earth or reclining in the earth.

In the Orphic tradition she emerged from Hydros, the Primordial Waters. According to Hesiod however, she emerged fully formed after Chaos at the moment of creation:

"ἦ τοι μὲν πρώτιστα Χάος γένετ᾽, αὐτὰρ ἔπειτα	"In truth at first Chaos came to be,
Γαῖ᾽ εὐρύστερνος, πάντων ἕδος ἀσφαλὲς αἰεὶ	but next wide-bosomed Earth, the ever-sure foundation
ἀθανάτων, οἳ ἔχουσι κάρη νιφόεντος Ὀλύμπου,	of all the deathless ones who hold the peaks of snowy Olympus, and dim
Τάρταρά τ᾽ ἠερόεντα μυχῷ χθονὸς εὐρυοδείης,"	Tartarus in the depth of the wide-pathed Earth,"

Gaia gave birth to Uranus (The Sky), Pontus (The Sea), and The Ourea (The Mountains). With Uranus, Gaia produced the Twelve Titans: Iapetus, Oceaus, Tethys, Hyperion, Theia, Coeus, Phoebe, Cronus, Rhea, Themis, Mnemosyne, and Crius. The Twelve Titans were followed by the one-eyed giants the Cyclopes: Brontes (Thunder), Sterops (Lightning), and Arges (Flash), and then the hundred handed giants, the Hecatoncheires: Cottus, Bruareus, and Gyges, and then the Meliae (Ash Tree Nymphs), the Giants, and the Erinyes (The Furies).

Hades (The Underworld and the Dead)

Greek Name(s): Ἀιδης, Haidês, Hades
Roman Name(s): Dis Pater, Orcus, Pluto

Hades is the Olympian god of the Dead, and the King of the Underworld, the unseen realm to which the souls of the dead go upon leaving the world. He presides over funeral rites and defends the right of the dead to due burial. He is depicted holding a bident, a helm or cap of invisibility, and with Cerberus the dog standing by his side (some say that Cerberus has three heads, some say fifty).

After the ten year war known as the Titanomachy and the defeat and overthrow of the Titans by the Olympians, Hades claimed joint rulership over the cosmos with his Olympian brothers Zeus and Poseidon. They drew lots to decide which of the realms they would rule. Zeus had the sky, Poseidon had the sea, and Hades had the Underworld, with which his name became synonymous.

For the Romans, the ruler of the Underworld was originally known as Orcus or Dis Pater (Rex Infernus = the King of Hell), similar to the Etruscan god Aite. These were merged into Pluto, which was a latinisation of Plouton meaning the rich one, a euphemistic title that the Greeks gave to Hades out of a superstitious aversion to mentioning his actual name.

Hades abducted Persephone and made her his wife and Queen of the Underworld. Persephone's mother Demeter was devastated by this abduction and asserted that the earth would be barren until she saw her daughter again. Zeus proposed a compromise whereby Persephone would have her time divided between the underworld and the earth and Mount Olympus, to which Hades agreed.

Persephone's return to the earth every year coincides with the retreat of the barren winter and the arrival of spring and the return of vegetation and grain crops.

Harmonia (Harmony and Concord)

Greek Name(s): Ἁρμονία, Harmonia, Harmonia
Roman Name(s): Concordia

Harmonia is the Olympian goddess of harmony and concord. Harmonia presides over marital harmony, soothing strife and discord. This later expanded to represent a more abstract sense of harmony, as a goddess who presided over the greater cosmic balance (depicted above allegorically balancing on one foot). Her opposite is the goddess Eris (Discordia).

She is the offspring of an adulterous affair between Aphrodite (Love) and Ares (War). Aphrodite's husband Hephaestus punished Aphrodite and Ares by catching them in a net, which he then showed to all the gods to ridicule.

Diodorus Siculus (5.8.42) alternatively suggests that Harmonia was born of Zeus and Electra, the Pleiad star nymph of Mount Saon on the island of Samothrace in the north Aegean Sea.

Harmonia was awarded to Cadmus, the hero and founder of the city of Thebes, in a wedding attended by the gods. Hephaestus never forgave Aphrodite for her betrayal, and presented Harmonia with a cursed necklace, which doomed her descendants to endless tragedy.

After a string of catastrophes the couple emigrated to Illyria where they battled various local tribes to form a new kingdom. They were later transformed into serpents by the gods and carried off to the Islands of the Blessed in Elysium to live in peace.

Hebe (Eternal Youth, and Forgiveness)

Greek Name(s): Ἥβη, Hêbê, Hebe
Roman Name(s): Juventas

Hebe is the Olympian goddess of eternal youth, the prime of life, and forgiveness. The youngest of the gods, she is often given the epithet *Ganymeda* meaning gladdening princess. Her Roman equivalent is Juventas. She is also the cupbearer to the gods of Olympus, whom she serves ambrosia and nectar (the food and drink of the gods). The astrological symbol for Hebe or Juventas is a cup or goblet. Hebe's counterpart is the daimon Geras (Old Age).

She is often depicted offering a cup to her father Zeus in the form of an eagle. Eagles were symbolically connected to immortality and the folklore belief that the eagle, like the phoenix, is able to renew itself to a youthful state.

The people of Sicyon worshipped Hebe as a goddess of forgiveness or mercy. This association with forgiveness and mercy alongside that of eternal youth, hints at a more complex symbolic relationship between forgiveness and longer life, and its implied symmetrical opposite, containing the moral message that lack of forgiveness or mercy shortens life.

Hebe has the ability to restore youth to mortals, a power that none of the other gods appear to have, as in Ovid's Metamorphoses, where some of the gods lament the aging of their favoured mortals.

Hebe is the daughter of Zeus & Hera, and the divine wife of Heracles (Roman: Hercules). After Heracles and Hebe ascended to the heavens at Olympus, they produced two sons Anicetus and Alexiares, demigods who presided over the defence and fortification of towns and citadels. They were also the gatekeepers of Olympus.

Hecate (Magic, Spells, the Moon, and Crossroads)

Greek Name(s): Ἑκατη, Ἑκατα, Hekatê, Hekata, Hecate, Hecata
Roman Name(s): Trivia

Hecate is the Titan goddess of magic, spells, the moon, the night, crossroads, and ghosts.

She is often depicted holding a pair of torches, a key, snakes, or accompanied by dogs.

In later periods she became depicted as three-formed or triple-headed.

The Romans knew her as Trivia (three-ways, a crossroads of three ways).

In magical traditions, she is referred to as The Triple Goddess.

She was worshipped in ancient Athens as a protector of the household along with Zeus, Hestia, Hermes, and Apollo.

She also took on the role of a saviour, a mother of angels, and mother and saviour of the Cosmic World Soul (Anima Mundi = the soul of the world).

Hecate's associations with three-way crossroads, the night time, and the moon, are combined in the astrological symbols which represent her. Perhaps the most well-known of these is the symbol of the triple-moon, a conjunction of three phases of the moon side by side: a waxing moon, a full moon, and waning moon. These three stages of the moon were equated to three stages of womanhood: maiden, mother, and crone (old woman).

Hecate was associated with borders, city walls, doorways, and crossroads. This association extended to realms outside or beyond the world of the living, and the transitions between those worlds.

She had the power to protect from spirits, but she could also decide not to intervene, or actively drive the spirits towards unfortunate individuals who were to be punished.

Hecate is the daughter of Perses (Destruction) and Asteria (The Starry One). Hesiod writes:

"γείνατο δ' Ἀστερίην εὐώνυμον, ἥν ποτε Πέρσης
ἠγάγετ' ἐς μέγα δῶμα φίλην κεκλῆσθαι ἄκοιτιν.
ἣ δ' ὑποκυσαμένη Ἑκάτην τέκε, τὴν περὶ πάντων
Ζεὺς Κρονίδης τίμησε"

"Also she bore Asteria of happy name,
whom Perses
once led to his great house to be called his dear wife.
And she conceived and bore Hecate whom
Zeus the son of Cronos honored above all."

Helios (The Sun)

Greek Name(s): Ἥλιος, Hêlios, Helius, Helios
Roman Name(s): Sol, Sol Indiges, Sol Invictus

Helios is the Titan god of the sun. He is sometimes given his father's name Hyperion (the one above) as an epithet, and sometimes Phaethon (the shining one). His mother is Theia (The Shining Ether) who is also known as Euryphaessa (wide-shining) and Aethra (blue sky, ether).

Helios is the brother of Eos (The Dawn) and Selene (The Moon). Hesiod writes:

"θεία δ' Ἥλιόν τε μέγαν λαμπράν τε Σελήνην Ἠῶ θ', ἣ πάντεσσιν ἐπιχθονίοισι φαείνει ἀθανάτοις τε θεοῖσι, τοὶ οὐρανὸν εὐρὺν ἔχουσι, γείναθ' ὑποδμηθεῖσ' Ὑπερίονος ἐν φιλότητι."

"and Theia was subject in love to Hyperion, and bore great Helios and clear Selene and Eos who shines upon all that are on earth and upon the deathless gods who live in the wide heaven"

Due to his position above the earth, Helios is believed to be an all-seeing witness who is invoked to oversee sworn oaths. He is commonly depicted in art wearing a radiant crown and riding a quadriga (a chariot drawn by four horses, sometimes winged horses).

At the eastern edge of the world, Helios lives in a golden palace in Oceanus, the river that encircles the earth, personified by the god Oceanus. Each morning his sister Eos (The Dawn) announces his arrival and he travels across the sky to the west. Some sources say that Eos accompanies him on his entire journey.

At the end of the day when he reaches the land of the Hesperides in the west, he then descends into a golden cup which takes him through the northern streams of Oceanus back to his home and rising place in the east.

He was worshipped on the island of Rhodes (where he was the patron god), Corinth, and the greater Corinthia region. The Colossus of Rhodes, one of the Seven Wonders of the Ancient World, was a gigantic statue of Helios that stood 33 metres high at the port of Rhodes from 280 BCE until it was destroyed in an earthquake in 226 BCE.

According to one myth, Helios gave permission for his mortal son Phaethon to drive his chariot across the sky for one day. Despite many warnings of the seriousness of the task and the possible dangers, Phaethon's journey is a disastrous as he cannot control the horses. Zeus struck Phaethon with a lightning bolt to stop him from riding too close to the earth and burning it or riding too far away from the earth and freezing it beyond salvation. This is a cautionary tale of unheeded warnings, and their consequences, which are often outside of the control of those who warn of them.

Hemera (The Day)

Greek Name(s): Ἡμερα, Hêmera, Hemera
Roman Name(s): Dies

Hemera is the Primordial personification of the day. She is the daughter or Erebus (The Darkness) and Nyx (The Night), and the sister and wife of Aether (Heavenly Light). Hesiod writes:

"ἐκ Χάεος δ' Ἔρεβός τε μέλαινά τε Νὺξ ἐγένοντο·	"From Chaos came forth Erebus and black Night;
Νυκτὸς δ' αὖτ' Αἰθήρ τε καὶ Ἡμέρη ἐξεγένοντο,	but of Night were born Aether and Hemera,
οὓς τέκε κυσαμένη Ἐρέβει φιλότητι μιγεῖσα.	whom she conceived with Erebus.
Γαῖα δέ τοι πρῶτον μὲν ἐγείνατο ἶσον ἑαυτῇ"	and bore from union in love"

In the evening Hemera's mother Nyx (The Night) draws her dark veil of Erebus (The Darkness) across the sky, obscuring Aether from the earth and bringing about the night. In the morning Hemera disperses the mists of the night and reveals the shining blue Aether of the day.

Hesiod regards Hemera as a divine substance rather than an anthropomorphic goddess. This is a common theme of difference between the Primordials (divine substance) and the successive generations of Titans and Olympians (anthropomorphic).

Over time Hemera became more and more identified with Eos (The Dawn), until finally Hemera's role was replaced by Eos, and they became identified as one and the same.

Hephaestus (Blacksmith of the Gods)

Greek Name(s): Ἥφαιστος, Hêphaistos, Hephaestus
Roman Name(s): Vulcanus, Vulcan

Hephaestus is the Olympian god of fire, smithery, craftsmen, metallurgy, metalworking, stonemasonry, and sculpture.

He is often depicted as a bearded man holding tools of smithery such as a hammer or a pair of tongs.

He is a master-crafter capable of creating objects with special properties.

He serves as blacksmith to the gods and makes all of their equipment, thrones, and weapons.

He designed Hermes's winged helmet and sandals, Aphrodite's girdle, Helios's chariot, and Eros's bow.

In later accounts he worked with the help of the Cyclopes, among them Brontes (Thunder), Stereops (Lightning), and Arges (Flash), who famously designed Zeus's thunderbolt.

According to Homer's Iliad, Hephaestus built a number of automatons made of metal to work for him or for others. This included tripods with golden wheels, able to move at his wish in and out of the assembly of the hall of the celestials:

"τρίποδας γὰρ ἐείκοσι πάντας ἔτευχεν ἑστάμεναι περὶ τοῖχον ἐϋσταθέος μεγάροιο,

χρύσεα δέ σφ᾽ ὑπὸ κύκλα ἑκάστῳ πυθμένι θῆκεν,
ὄφρά οἱ αὐτόματοι θεῖον δυσαίατ᾽ ἀγῶνα

ἠδ᾽ αὖτις πρὸς δῶμα νεοίατο θαῦμα ἰδέσθαι.
οἳ δ᾽ ἤτοι τόσσον μὲν ἔχον τέλος, οὔατα δ᾽ οὔ πω"

"for he was fashioning tripods, twenty in all, to stand around the wall of his well-builded hall,
and golden wheels had he set beneath the base of each
that of themselves they might enter the gathering
of the gods at his wish and again return to his house, a wonder to behold"

Hephaestus is the son of Hera, and although it is not certain that Zeus is his father, Zeus is described in such a way. In one account Hera rejected Hephaestus and threw him from the heavens because of his physical impairment at birth. Hephaestus fell into the ocean and was cared for and raised by Thetis and Eurynome. Another account suggests that Zeus threw Hephaestus out of the heavens for obstructing his advances towards Hera. Hephaestus fell for a whole day and landed on the island of Lemnos, where he was taught to be a master craftsman by the Sintians, an ancient tribe native to the area, and Hephaestus's physical disability was due to the fall.

Hera (Queen of the Gods)

Greek Name(s): Ἥρη, Hêrê, Hera
Roman Name(s): Juno

Hera is the Olympian queen of the gods and of Mount Olympus, the goddess of marriage, the sky and the stars of heaven, and the protector of women. She is depicted as a beautiful woman wearing a crown and holding a sceptre tipped with a lotus, and accompanied by a lion, a cuckoo, or a hawk.

Hera's sacred animal is the peacock, and the astrological symbols for Hera and her Roman equivalent Juno represent a peacock with a cross at the bottom.

She is a dignified matronly figure, upright, enthroned, wearing a high cylindrical crown known as a *polos* or a diadem, and veiled as a married woman.

Hera is known for her jealous and vengeful nature in punishing those who wrong her, particularly Zeus's many adulterous lovers and illegitimate offspring.

She is the patron goddess of lawful marriage who presides over weddings, blesses and legalises marital unions, and protects women during childbirth. She is sometimes shown holding a pomegranate as an emblem of immortality.

Before Hera's marriage to Zeus, she was a maternal goddess associated with cattle, given the epithet Boôpis by Homer translated as cow-eyed. This is similar to the Ancient Egyptian goddess Hathor who is also a maternal goddess associated with cattle.

Her name can be traced back to tablets from the Mycenaean Greek period (1600-1300 BCE) as *E-ra*, or *E-ra-i*. The two main temples and centres of her cult were the Heraion of Samos, and the Heraion of Argos, both of which were constructed in around the 8th century BCE. She was celebrated in the festival of Heraia. Homeric Hymn no.12 to Hera reads:

"Ἥρην ἀείδω χρυσόθρονον, ἣν τέκε Ῥείη,

ἀθανάτων βασίλειαν, ὑπείροχον εἶδος ἔχουσαν,
Ζην`-ὸς ἐριγδούποιο κασιγνήτην ἄλοχόν τε,

κυδρήν, ἣν πάντες μάκαρες κατὰ μακρὸν Ὄλυμπον
ἀζόμενοι τίουσιν ὁμῶς Διὶ τερπικεραύνῳ."

"I sing of golden-throned Hera whom Rhea bare.
Queen of the immortals is she, surpassing all in beauty:
she is the sister and the wife of loud-thundering Zeus,
the glorious one whom all the blessed throughout high Olympus
reverence and honor even as Zeus who delights in thunder."

Hermes (The Divine Messenger)

Greek Name(s): Ἑρμης, Hermês, Hermes
Roman Name(s): Mercurius, Mercury

Hermes is the Olympian god of athletes, boundaries, commerce, cunning, hospitality, language, merchants, messages, oratory, roads, shepherds, speed, thieves, travellers, and wit.

He is the son of Zeus and Maia (one of the Pleiades). He also serves as a divine messenger for his father Zeus.

His winged sandals (Greek: *pedila*, Roman: *talaria*) allow him to move quickly and freely between the worlds of the mortal and the divine. He also plays the role of a guide who transfers souls to the afterlife.

He is depicted holding a winged staff entwined with two snakes called a caduceus. The astrological symbol for Hermes, or his Roman counterpart Mercurius (Mercury), is a representation of this caduceus, a powerful symbol that is documented among the Babylonians as far back as 3500 BCE. This symbol was also used in depictions of the Mesopotamian god Ningishzida, who like Hermes is a mediator between humans and the divine.

Hermes is sometimes depicted wearing a *petasos* (Latin: *petasus*), a type of rural sun hat which was representative of rural Greeks. Sometimes this hat was winged, and later the wings rose directly from his head, influenced by the equivalent Etruscan god Turms.

From 800 BCE to around 480 BCE he was depicted as an older bearded man dressed as a traveller, herald, or shepherd. This image remained on the boundary markers, roadside markers, and votive offerings which were called *Hermai*, pillar-like in shape with the head of Hermes at the top. These Hermai later appeared as grave monuments, symbolising Hermes's role as a transporter of souls to the Underworld. He was later depicted as a young athletic and clean-shaven man.

In Ptolemaic Egypt, the Egyptian god Thoth was identified with Hermes and the two gods became worshipped as one at the Temple of Thoth in Khemenu, a city which became known as Hermopolis. This led to Hermes being associated with translation and interpretation, or more generally a god of knowledge and learning. In the temple at Esna on the west bank of the Nile the epithet Thoth the great, the great, the great was applied to Hermes at around 172 BCE. This led to Hermes being referred to as *Hermes Trismegistus* (the thrice-greatest Hermes).

The name Hermes Trismegistus, known in Latin as *Mercurius ter Maximus* (Mercury the three times greatest) and was said to be the author of the *Hermetica*, a widely diverse collection of ancient and medieval texts that are the basis for the philosophical system known as *Hermeticism*. In the field of natural philosophy, particularly alchemy, it was often referred to as The Hermetic Art.

The Hesperides (Nymphs of the Sunset)

Greek Name(s): Ἑσπερις, Ἑσπεριδες, Hesperis, Hesperides, Hesperid, Hesperides
Roman Name(s): Vesperae

The Hesperides are the Primordial nymphs of the evening and the golden light of the sunset. Their name comes from the ancient Greek *hésperos* (ἕσπερος), and the Latin *vesper* meaning evening, the evening star, the west, or western, the west being the domain of the sunset.

Hesiod describes the Hesperides as the daughters of Nyx with no father. Hyginus and Cicero name Erebus as their father. Their number varies between three, four and seven. Hesiod gives their four names as Aegle, Erytheia, Hesperia, and Arethusa.

The earliest legends describe the Garden of the Hesperides as being in the extreme west, on the river Oceanus that encircles the earth, personified by the Titan god Oceanus. Some sources suggest that their garden is near the Atlas Mountains in North Africa. According to Pliny the Elder, the garden is located at Lixus, Morocco. The geographer Strabo, in his book *Geographika,* suggests Tartessos, the location of an ancient civilisation on the south of the Iberian Peninsula spanning southern Portugal and southern Spain.

The Hesperides are also depicted as heralds of the bridal night. According to legend they attended the wedding of Thetis (Nereid of the Sea) and the hero Peleus (King of Phthia).

The Hesperides were entrusted with the care of the tree of the golden apples that Gaia presented to Hera on the day of her wedding with Zeus. Quintus Smyrnaeus in his Fall of Troy describes them serving ambrosia (the food of the gods) in golden chalices.

Hestia (The Sacred Fire)

Greek Name(s): Ἑστία, Hestia, Hestia
Roman Name(s): Vesta

Hestia is the Olympian goddess of the hearth, the fireplace, the symbolic focal point of the home, and by extension, the home in general, domesticity, and community.

The astrological symbols for Hestia, or her Roman equivalent Vesta, represent a hearthstone, a fire, or a flame.

She is the daughter of the Titans Cronus and Rhea. Along with four of her five siblings (Demeter, Hades, Hera, and Poseidon), she was devoured by her father Cronus as an infant due to Cronus's fear of being overthrown by his offspring. Hestia's youngest brother Zeus forced Cronus to vomit them all back up from his stomach.

In the Homeric Hymn to Aphrodite, Hestia is the first to be born and the last to be yielded up again, and as such, she is the eldest and the youngest of the siblings simultaneously. When the Titans were finally defeated and overthrown, Hestia then became one of the Twelve Olympians, the new rulers of the cosmos.

Poseidon and Apollo both declared their love for Hestia and vied for her hand in marriage, but Hestia rejected them both. She swore a great oath to Zeus that she would remain a virgin and never marry. In the Homeric Hymn to Aphrodite, Aphrodite is described as having no power over Hestia.

Hestia was a very important goddess in ancient Greece and Rome, with public hearths serving as a focal point for towns and cities. As the goddess of sacred and sacrificial fire, Hestia received the first offering in every household, and the first and last libations of wine.

Founders of city states or colonies would ask for permission from their mother city, and whenever a new colony was established, a flame from Hestia's public hearth would be carried to the new settlement.

Hestia is traditionally depicted simply wearing a cloak and a head veil, sometimes with a staff in her hand, next to a fire. Her throne is plain and wooden, with a white woollen cushion.

Every private and public hearth was regarded as a sanctuary of Hestia, and a portion of the sacrifices offered to any gods belonged to her.

In the Roman tradition the priestesses of Vesta, known as Vestal Virgins, administered the temple and kept the flame burning. As the keeper of the flame at Olympus, Hestia is considered to be the first Vestal Virgin.

The Horae (The Hours and the Seasons)

Greek Name(s): Ὡρα, Ὡραι, Hôra, Hôrai, Hora, Horae
Roman Name(s): Horae

The Horae are the Olympian goddesses of the hours, seasons, and natural portions of time. They preside over the heavenly constellations by which the year is measured.

They were particularly honoured by farmers who planted and tended their crops in time with the rising and setting of the stars and constellations on the celestial equator.

According to Hesiod, they are the daughters of Zeus and Themis, and the half-sisters of the Moirai (The Fates). Quintus Smyrnaeus suggests that they are the daughters of Helios (The Sun) and Selene (The Moon).

Their names and number vary depending on the sources. Hesiod names three of them as Eunomia (good order and good pasture), Dike (natural law), and Eirene (peace). Pausanias names Thallo (spring, blooming), Carpo (autumn, harvest, fruit), Auxo or Auxesia (Growth), and Damia (Earth).

In later times they came to represent good order, natural law, and justice more generally. They are the ministers of Zeus who guard the gates of Olympus, promote the fertility of the earth, sending down various kinds of weather. The course of the seasons is symbolically described as the dance of the Horae.

Thallo, the bringer of Spring, is said to accompany Persephone on her ascent from the Underworld, and the Orphic Hymn phrase The chamber of the Horae opens is equivalent to The spring is coming.

Hydros (The Primordial Waters)

Greek Name(s): Ὑδρος, Hydros, Hydros
Roman Name(s): Hydrus

In the Orphic tradition Hydros is the Primordial personification of the Primordial Waters, one of the first entities to emerge at the beginning of creation.

Out of Hydros emerged mud, which solidified into Gaia (Earth). Gaia and Hydros then produced Chronos (Time) and Ananke (Necessity) who in serpentine form coiled themselves around the Cosmic Egg or World Egg, causing it to split apart.

Out of this egg hatched Phanes (Protogonus) the god of creation, who divided the cosmos into the heavens, the earth, the sea, and the sky.

After their part in the act of creation, Chronos and Ananke then circled the cosmos, driving the rotation of the heavens and the eternal passage of time.

Later Orphic Rhapsodies discard the figures of Chronos and Ananke and instead describe Phanes as being born directly from Hydros and Gaia.

Hydros is identified with Oceanus, the fresh water river that encircles the earth. His consort Thesis is likewise identified with Oceanus's consort Tethys.

Hygieia (Health, Healing, and Hygiene)

Greek Name(s): Ὑγεια, Hygeia, Hygieia
Roman Name(s): Salus, Valetudo

Hygieia is the Olympian goddess of good health, cleanliness, and sanitation. Her name is where the English word hygiene comes from. She is one of the Asclepiades (children of Asclepius).

She has four sisters: Panacea (universal remedy), Iaso (recuperation), Aceso (healing), and Aegle (good health). Their mother is Epione (the goddess of soothing pain).

Hygieia is often depicted holding a large serpent in her arms and a small bowl in her hand called a *patera* or a *phiale* (a shallow dish used in religious ceremonies), which she uses to feed the serpent.

The Roman counterpart to Hygieia is either Salus (safety, salvation, or welfare), or Valetudo (health). The astrological symbols for Hygieia and her Roman counterparts are a caduceus (a staff entwined with two snakes), a staff entwined with one snake, a snake and a star, or a bowl entwined by a snake.

The worship of Hygieia is closely associated with the cult of Asclepius, located in healing temples called Asclepieia across the Greek and Roman world. While Asclepius is more directly associated with healing, Hygieia is associated with the prevention of sickness and the continuation of good health.

Devotees would attend the temples seeking spiritual and physical healing, and some would sleep in the temple with the expectation that they would be visited by Asclepius or one of his children in their dream, which would be reported to a priest who would interpret the dream and prescribe a cure.

Hyperion (Heavenly Light)

Greek Name(s): Ὑπεριων, Hyperiôn, Hyperion
Roman Name(s): Hyperion

Hyperion is the Titan god of heavenly light. Hyperion's name translates as watching from above or he who goes above from the Greek words *hyper* and *ion*.

He is one of the sons of Uranus (The Sky), and Gaia (Earth), and the father of the lights of heaven Eos (The Dawn), Helios (The Sun), and Selene (The Moon). His wife is Theia (the goddess of the shining blue of the sky). Hesiod in his Theogony (line 371) writes:

"θεία δ' Ἡέλιόν τε μέγαν λαμπράν τε Σελήνην Ἠῶ θ', ἣ πάντεσσιν ἐπιχθονίοισι φαείνει ἀθανάτοις τε θεοῖσι, τοὶ οὐρανὸν εὐρὺν ἔχουσι, γείναθ' ὑποδμηθεῖσ' Ὑπερίονος ἐν φιλότητι."	"and Theia was subject in love to Hyperion, and bore great Helios and clear Selene and Eos who shines upon all that are on earth and upon the deathless gods who live in the wide heaven"

Led by Cronus, Hyperion and his brothers conspired against their father Uranus, laying an ambush for him as he descended to Gaia in order to lay with her. They waited at the four corners of the world and seized hold of Uranus, and held him down while Cronus, who waited in the centre, castrated Uranus with the stone sickle that Gaia had made especially, and then threw his severed genitals into the sea. The brothers personified the great pillars holding heaven and earth apart. Hyperion was the east, Coeus was the north, Iapetus was the west, and Crius was the south. After the Titans were overthrown by Zeus, Hyperion and his brothers (except Oceanus) were imprisoned in Tartarus. According to Pindar and Aeschylus, the Titans were eventually released from Tartarus because of Zeus's clemency.

Hypnos (Sleep)

Greek Name(s): Ὕπνος, Hypnos, Hypnus, Hypnos
Roman Name(s): Somnus

Hypnos is the Primordial personification of sleep, and his name is where the word hypnosis comes from (*hypnos* = sleep + *osis* = condition).

His Roman equivalent is Somnus, and in some sources he is the fatherless son of Nyx (The Night), while other sources state that his father is Erebus (The Darkness).

Next to his twin brother Thanatos (Peaceful Death), Hypnos lives in a cave in the Underworld (Hades) where the river Lethe (Forgetfulness) comes from, where day and night meet, but where no sunlight or sound enters. His bed is made of ebony, and at the entrance to his cave there are poppies growing, along with other sleep inducing plants.

Hypnos and Thanatos are the subject of a painting by John William Waterhouse called Sleep and His Half-Brother Death, depicting the two figures side by side. The lighter figure in the foreground is Sleep (Hypnos) holding poppies in his hands, and the darker figure in the background is Death (Thanatos).

Hypnos, and other descendents of Nyx such as Thanatos and Morpheus, have long been metaphorically associated with trance, sleep, and death, and in art they have long been depicted with poppies, scattering poppies, or with poppies nearby.

With the revival of classical learning, this iconography continued in paintings from the Renaissance period onwards. The Pre-Raphaelite influenced painting Night and Sleep by Evelyn de Morgan in 1878 features Nyx and Hypnos figuratively travelling across the sky from east to west (left to right), scattering poppies as they go.

Hypnos's wife is Pasithea, one of the youngest of the Charites who was promised to him by Hera, the Queen of the Gods in return for him causing Zeus to fall asleep, affecting the course of the Trojan War in Hera's favour.

Pasithea's name has been translated by breaking it down into two elements *pasis* = acquired + *thea* = sight or vision. With the name meaning acquired sight, it has been interpreted that she is a source of hallucinations or visions, along with rest and relaxation.

Hypnos and Pasithea produced the Oneiroi, the thousand dream spirits, of whom Morpheus (The Shaper of Dreams) is their leader. The Romans knew the Oneiroi as the Somnia or dream shapes, who appear in dreams mimicking many forms. Morpheus appears in human form, Icelos or Phobetor appear as beasts, and Phantasos appears as inanimate objects.

Iapetus (Mortality and the Mortal Life Span)

Greek Name(s): *Ιαπετος*, Iapetos, Iapetus, Japetus
Roman Name(s): Iapetus

Iapetus is the Titan god of mortality and the mortal life span. His name means to pierce with a spear. He is the son of Uranus (The Sky) and Gaia (The Earth).

Led by Cronus, Iapetus and his brothers conspired against their father Uranus, laying an ambush for him as he descended to Gaia in order to lay with her.

They waited at the four corners of the world and seized hold of Uranus, and held him down while Cronus, who waited in the centre, castrated Uranus with the stone sickle that Gaia had made especially, and then threw his severed genitals into the sea.

The brothers personified the great pillars holding heaven and earth apart. Iapetus was the west, Hyperion was the east, Coeus was the north, and Crius was the south.

After the Titans were overthrown by Zeus, Hyperion and his brothers (except Oceanus) were imprisoned in Tartarus. According to Pindar and Aeschylus, the Titans were eventually released from Tartarus because of Zeus's clemency.

According to Hesiod, Iapetus and Clymene together produced Atlas (The Holder of the Sky), Prometheus (Foresight), Epithemeus (Hindsight), and Menoetius (Violent Anger and Rash Action).

Iris (The Rainbow Messenger)

Greek Name(s): Ιρις, Iris, Iris
Roman Name(s): Arcus, Iris

Iris is the goddess of the rainbow and the messenger of the Olympian gods. She is often described as the handmaiden and personal messenger of Hera. The ancient Greek name Îris (Ἶρις) translates both as rainbow and the halo of the moon. She is the daughter of Thaumas (a Primordial personification of the sea), and Electra (one of the three thousand Oceanids, water-nymphs).

Iris is depicted as a winged young woman, sometimes carrying a caduceus (a symbol of a divine messenger, a staff entwined with two snakes), and sometimes a pitcher which she uses to serve the gods nectar or water. She is the consort of Zephyrus (The West Wind), and together they produced Pothos, one of the Erotes (Love Spirits) who accompanies Aphrodite.

Iris has the power to travel with the speed of the wind from one end of the world to the other, and into the depths of the Kingdom of the Sea and the Underworld. Some say that Iris travels on the rainbow when delivering messages from the gods to mortals on earth.

There are no known temples, shrines, or sanctuaries dedicated to Iris, nor any festivals held in her honour. She does appear to have been worshipped or at least sacrificed to by the people of Delos, offering her a cheesecake called *basyniae*, a type of cake of wheatflour, suet, and honey boiled together.

Iris has been given many poetic titles and epithets, including golden winged, swift footed, wind-swift footed, dewy, daughter of Thaumas, wondrous one, storm-footed, and storm-swift.

The Keres (The Spirits of Death)

Greek Name(s): *Κηρ, Κηρες*, Kêr, Kêres, Keres
Roman Name(s): Letum, Tenebrae

The Keres are the female spirits (*daimones*) of violent or cruel death, either on the battlefield, by accident, by murder, or by ravaging disease. They are depicted as women with fangs and talons wearing bloody garments. They are the agents of the Moirai (The Fates, who measure out the life thread of every person) and Moros (Doom, who drives people toward their inevitable destruction).

The Keres are cravers of blood, and fight amongst each other to feast upon the dying, tearing the souls free from the mortally wounded bodies, sending them on their way to Hades (The Underworld). The Olympians are sometimes described standing by their favourites on the battlefield beating the Keres away from them.

Hesiod describes three types of Keres, *kakoi* (evils), *nosoi* (sicknesses and diseases), and *lugra* (banes), and that they are the daughters of Nyx (The Night) with no father. Other sources add Erebus (The Darkness) as their father. From Cicero, the Romans knew them as *Tenebrae* (the darknesses) or *Leta* (the deaths).

Dating back to the 5th century CE, vases depicting the Keres were believed to have been part of apotropaic rites and rituals to ward off evil and keep the Keres away. The word apotropaic comes from the ancient Greek *apotrópaios* (ἀποτρόπαιος), from *apó* (ἀπό) = away + *trópos* (τρόπος) = turn), to turn things away, as in turning away evil.

Melpomene (Muse of Tragedy)

Greek Name(s): *Μελπομενη*, Melpomenê, Melpomene
Roman Name(s): Melpomene

Melpomene is the Olympian Muse of tragedy and the chorus. She is one of the nine Muses who dwell at either Mount Helicon or Mount Parnassus, the daughters of Zeus, god of the sky, and Mnemosyne (the goddess of Memory).

Her name is from the Greek verb *melpô* or *melpomai* meaning to celebrate with dance and song. She is often depicted holding a tragic mask, a sword, sometimes wearing a wreath of ivy, or wearing cothurnus boots or buskins, a thick soled boot worn by actors in Greek tragedy. She is described as singing songs of mourning for people of note after they die, particularly poets.

Diodorus Siculus in his Library of History (4.7.1) describes how people assign special abilities to the Muses representing different branches of the liberal arts, such as poetry, song, dance, study of the stars, and others:

> *"Μελπομένην δ' ἀπὸ τῆς μελῳδίας, δι' ἧς τοὺς ἀκούοντας ψυχαγωγεῖσθαι,"*
> "Melpomene, from the melody by which she charms the souls of her listeners,"

According to some accounts (Apollodorus, Lycophron, and Hyginus), Melpomene gave birth to the Sirens. The father of the Sirens is Achelous, an ancient river god in Aetolia in western Greece. The Sirens inherited their mother's voice which, according to legend, they used to lure sailors toward their ruin on the rocks known as the Sirenum Scopuli.

Mnemosyne (Memory and Remembrance)

Greek Name(s): *Μνημοσυνη*, Mnêmosynê, Mnemosyne
Roman Name(s): Mnemosyne, Moneta

Mnemosyne is the Titan goddess of memory and remembrance, and the inventor of language and words. She represents the memorising of the stories of history, myth, and poetry before the introduction of writing.

She is the daughter of Uranus (The Sky) and Gaia (The Earth). Hyginus suggests that Aether may be her father instead of Uranus.

Mnemosyne gave birth to the nine Muses who originally represented all of the liberal arts collectively, including poetry, with Zeus as their father.

From the 5th to the 4th centuries BCE onwards, the Muses began to be recognised, identified, and assigned more specific aspects of the liberal arts individually.

By her association with the Muses, Mnemosyne is also associated with music and poetry. Some sources identify Mnemosyne with one of the Elder Muses or Boeotian Muses known as Mneme (literally memory). Her sisters were variously named as Melete (practise), Aiode (song), and Thelxinoe (mind charming).

The name of the Roman goddess Moneta is associated with Mnemosyne, which comes from the word *monere*, meaning to remind, to warn, or to instruct. Confusingly the name is also used as an epithet for the Roman goddess Juno (Hera), i.e. Juno Moneta.

The Moirai (The Three Fates)

Greek Name(s): *Μοιρα, Μοιραι*, Moira, Moirai, Moirai
Roman Name(s): Fatum, Fatae, Parcae

The Moirai are the three Primordial personifications of fate, often referred to as The Fates. They decide the fate and destiny of every human life. The Romans knew them as the Fatae, or the Parcae.

Clotho (*Κλωθώ*, Klotho) is the youngest of the fates known as the spinner. She spins the thread of each human life on her spindle, and also decides when each person is born. Her Roman equivalent is Nona.

Lachesis (*Λάχεσις*, Lákhesis) is the middle of the fates known as the dispenser of lots. She measures the thread of each human life as it leaves Clotho's spindle. She decides how long each thread of life will be. Her Roman equivalent is Decima.

Atropos (*Ἄτροπος*, Atropos) is the elder of the fates. She is known as the inflexible one or she who cannot be turned, and she chooses the manner of death and the ending of each human life by cutting their threads. Her Roman equivalent is Morta.

There are many different versions or accounts of their parentage, among them are Zeus and Themis, or Erebus & Nyx, etc. Plato in his Republic suggests that they are the daughters of Ananke (Necessity).

Moirai is the plural of Moira, which in ancient Greek means a share, a lot, or something apportioned, and so the Moirai assign every human their share or lot of fate and destiny.

Momus (Mockery, Satire, and Criticism)

Greek Name(s): *Μωμος*, Mômos, Momus, Momus
Roman Name(s): Momus

Momus is the Primordial personification of mockery, satire, blame, ridicule, scorn, complaint, and harsh criticism.

He is an important part of Greek and Roman culture as a symbol of that which exposes vices, follies, abuses, and shortcomings to ridicule.

In a civilised society this mockery and satire (and the freedom to practice it) is prized as a form of constructive social criticism, whereby individuals, corporations, governments, or society itself can be shamed into improvement.

Momus embodies the duality of harsh and unfair criticism on one hand, and holding power to account, or talking truth to power on the other hand.

Freedom comes with responsibility, and actions come with consequences, and so the cautionary tale is that Momus was expelled from the heavens by Zeus for ridiculing the gods.

As a spirit of criticism, Momus is also associated with fault-finding. Plato in his Republic describes the idea of something so perfect that even "Momus himself could not find fault with it".

The opposite of Momus is Eupheme (the goddess of Praise and Acclaim).

Moros (Impending Doom)

Greek Name(s): *Μορος*, Moros, *Ολεθρος*, Olethros
Roman Name(s): Fatum, Olethrus

Moros is the Primordial personification of doom, the personified spirit (*daimon*) of the impending force that drives mortals to their ultimate fate. His name translates as doom, fate, ruin, and calamity.

Also translating from the name Olethros (*Ολεθρος*) is the word bane, an archaic word of Old English origin meaning something which causes death, especially poison.

Among his siblings collectively known as the Children of Nyx are: the Moirai, the Three Fates, Thanatos (the god of peaceful death), and the Keres (the spirits of death on the battlefield).

Hesiod describes Moros as bring born of Nyx without a father, whereas Hyginus and Cicero name Erebus as his father.

Moros also has the power to enable mortals to foresee their impending fate. The Romans knew Moros as Fatum, and he is also known by the name Olethrus.

Aeschylus writes in Prometheus Bound that Prometheus gave humanity the spiritess (daimona) Elpis (Hope) or the spiritesses (daimones) Elpides (The Hopes) in order help them to ignore Moros.

Moros is also referred to as "the all-destroying god, who, even in the realm of Death, does not set his victim free".

Morpheus (The Shaper of Dreams)

Greek Name(s): *Μορφευς*, Morpheus, Morpheus
Roman Name(s): Morpheus

Morpheus is the Primordial personification of dreams, and the leader of the thousand dreams spirits known as the Oneiroi (the Somnia in the Roman tradition). His name translates as the Fashioner, or the Shaper, which comes from the ancient Greek word *morphé* or *morfí* (μορφή), meaning shape, form, or figure.

Morpheus is the son of Hypnos (the god of sleep), and Pasithea (the personification of relaxation, meditation, and hallucinations).

As well as representing sleep and dreams in general and leading the thousand dream spirits, Morpheus also shapes and forms the dreams of mortals, in which he has the power to appear in human guise to deliver messages from the gods.

His domain is Erebus, the Primordial darkness that encircles the world and fills the deep hollows of the earth.

The Roman poet Ovid is the first to name him in his narrative poem Metamorphoses as the son of Somnus (Hypnos). Morpheus appears in the tale of Ceyx and Alcyone, the Thessalian couple who committed hubris by sacrilegiously calling each other Zeus and Hera.

This angered Zeus, and so while Ceyx was at sea to consult an oracle, Zeus killed Ceyx with a thunderbolt. Soon afterwards Morpheus appeared to Alcyone in a dream disguised as her husband Ceyx to tell her the truth of what had happened. Alcyone in her grief threw herself into the sea, and out of compassion the gods transformed them both into halcyon birds (common kingfishers).

The opiate morphine gets its name from the god Morpheus. The use of opium from poppies (*papaver somniferum*) as a pain medication and a treatment of stomach complaints and other ailments dates back to ancient times, long before the ancient Greeks.

The amount of active ingredients (alkaloids) in opium has always varied considerably, historically making controlled dosage notoriously difficult. In 1804 the German pharmacist Friedrich Sertürner successfully isolated these alkaloids.

He hoped that by isolating the morphine and controlling the amount in each dose, the problems of overdose and addiction could be avoided. He first named it *morphium* after the god Morpheus because it had a tendency to cause sleep, and it later became known as *morphine.*

Gods and goddesses descended from Nyx, such as Morpheus, Hypnos, and Thanatos, have long been metaphorically associated with trance, sleep, and death, and in art they have long been depicted with poppies, scattering poppies, or with poppies nearby. With the revival of classical learning, this iconography continued in paintings from the Renaissance period onwards.

Nemesis (Divine Retributive Justice)

Greek Name(s): *Νεμεσις*, Nemesis, *Ῥαμνουσία*, Rhamnousia
Roman Name(s): Invidia, Invidentia, Nemesis, Rivalitas

Nemesis is the Primordial personification of retribution, retributive justice, vengeance, and punishment of hubris, arrogance before the gods, evil deeds, and ill-deserved good fortune. She is an agent of the moral reverence for natural law.

Her name means she who distributes or deals out what is due. She is a winged goddess depicted with a wide range of icons, such as an apple branch, balancing scales, a bridle, a dagger, a lash, a measuring rod, a rein, a sand-clock or timer, a sword, or a whip. The Romans knew her as Nemesis, but she was also referred to as Invidia or Invidentia (Jealousy), and Rivalitas (Rivalry).

Happiness and unhappiness is measured out by her, making sure that happiness is not too frequent or too excessive, to maintain equilibrium. She punishes and levels the balance by bringing about losses and suffering, sometimes as a check against the extravagant favours of the goddesses Tyche (Luck) or Fortuna (Fortune).

Hesiod and Pausanias both suggest that Nemesis was born of Nyx (The Night) with no father, whereas Hyginus and Cicero name Erebus as her father. Oceans and Zeus are also suggested as her father in other sources.

Nemesis is sometimes given the name Adrasteia (the inescapable) by the writers of Adrastus who according to Strabo built the first sanctuary of Nemesis on the river Asopus. She is also given the name Rhamnousia because of the temple dedicated to her at Rhamnos in Attica according to Pausanias.

Nike (Victory)

Greek Name(s): *Νικη*, Nikê, Nike
Roman Name(s): Victoria

Nike is the Olympian goddess of victory, both on the battlefield in times of war, and in any form of competition, athletic or otherwise, in times of peace. She is most commonly depicted with wings, wearing golden sandals, in flight or leaning forward holding a crown of victory in the form of a laurel wreath or a palm frond.

Sometimes she is described as an attribute of Athena with some statues depicting her standing in the palm of Athena's hand. She is also associated with Zeus as an attribute or an attendant, as she was the first among the gods to offer her allegiance to Zeus during the Titanomachy, the war against the Titans.

Hesiod, Apollodorus, and Hyginus state that Nike is the daughter of Pallas (the Titan god of battle and warcraft) and Styx (the goddess of the underworld river Styx). Her siblings are Zelus (Zeal), Cratos (Strength), and Bia (Force). By contrast, the Homeric Hymn to Ares suggests that Ares is Nike's father.

Nike appears on Greek painted vases with an *oinochoe* (bowl) and a *phiale* (cup) for libations, a *thymiaterion* (incense burner), an altar, and a lyre for the celebration of victory in song.

Nike's Roman counterpart is Victoria (victory), who was widely invoked during the Punic Wars against Ancient Carthage. She had her own temple on the Palatine Hill, the central and most ancient of the seven hills of Rome.

Nyx (The Night)

Greek Name(s): *Νυξ*, Nyx, Nyx
Roman Name(s): Nox

Nyx is the Primordial personification of the night who emerged at the dawn of creation.

She is the daughter of Chaos (The Void) and the sister of Erebus (The Darkness).

According to Hesiod, Nyx and Erebus produced Aether (The Bright Upper-Heavens), and Hemera (The Day).

In the Orphic tradition Nyx is the daughter and consort of Phanes (The Creator).

On her own, Nyx produced a number of dark spirits including Moros (Doom, Destiny), the Keres (Destruction, Death), Thanatos (Peaceful Death), Hypnos (Sleep), the Oneiroi (Dreams), Momus (Blame), Oizys (Pain, Distress), the Hesperides (Evening Nymphs), the Moirai (The Three Fates), Nemesis (Retribution), Apate (Deceit), Philotes (Love), Geras (Old Age), and Eris (Strife).

Every evening Nyx draws her veil of dark mists across the sky, obscuring the light of Aether. This dark veil is composed of the darkness of Erebus, which she either wears around her and then unfurls across the sky, or draws across the sky with a chariot.

Her opposite is her daughter Hemera (The Day) who scatters the mists of night each dawn, and thus Nyx and Hemera pass each other each day at the entrance to their dwelling in the Underworld.

One myth states that even Zeus was afraid of Nyx, because she was much older and more powerful than him. When Zeus was furious with Hypnos for having made him fall asleep at Hera's request, Hypnos fled to his mother Nyx for protection, and Zeus did not dare to pursue him any further for fear of upsetting or angering Nyx.

In ancient art Nyx is depicted as a winged goddess or a charioteer, crowned by a circle of dark mists, wearing a large black cloak or black robes. In 1883 the French painter William-Adolphe Bouguereau painted La Nuit, a then modern interpretation of Nyx. In his painting, Nyx has her black robe, and is also surrounded by four owls, which are commonly known as creatures of the night.

Nyx and her descendents, such as Morpheus, Hypnos, and Thanatos, have long been metaphorically associated with trance, sleep, and death, and in art they have long been depicted with poppies, scattering poppies, or with poppies nearby.

With the revival of classical learning, this iconography continued in paintings from the Renaissance period onwards. The Pre-Raphaelite influenced painting Night and Sleep by Evelyn de Morgan in 1878 features Nyx and Hypnos figuratively travelling across the sky from east to west (left to right), scattering poppies as they go.

Oceanus (The Earth-Encircling River)

Greek Name(s): Ωκεανος, Ôkeanos, Oceanus
Roman Name(s): Oceanus

Oceanus is the Titan god of the great river Oceanus that encircles the earth, the font of all the earth's fresh water, rivers, wells, springs, and rain clouds. He is one of the Twelve Titans, and the eldest son of Uranus (The Sky) and Gaia (The Earth).

Hesiod calls Oceanus "the perfect river" (τελήεντος ποταμοῖο, telíentos potamoío), and both Hesiod and Homer refer to Oceanus as "backflowing" (ἀψορρόου, apsorróou) because since he encircles the earth, he flows back into himself.

Oceanus and Tethys produced the three thousand Potamoi (The River Gods), and the three thousand Oceanids (Ocean Nymphs).

In Homer's Iliad (Book XIV), the story of the Deception of Zeus implies a tradition in which Oceanus and Tethys (rather than Uranus and Gaia as in Hesiod's Theogony) are the Primordials from whom all the others sprang forth.

In Homer's Odyssey, Oceanus is the father of the Aurai (Αυρα, Αυραι, Aura, Aurai), the nymphs of the breezes, whereas Quintus Smyrnaeus suggests they are born of Boreas (The North Wind).

Aristophanes names Oceanus and Tethys as the parents of the Nephelai (Νεφελη, Νεφελαι, Nephelê, Nephelai) who are the Oceanid nymphs of clouds and rain that rise from the river Oceanus and feed their brothers the Potamoi with fresh water and nourish the earth.

The Oneiroi (The Dream Spirits)

Greek Name(s): *Ονειρος, Ονειροι,* Oneiros, Oneiroi
Roman Name(s): Somnia

The Oneiroi (dreams) are the thousand dark winged dream spirits. They are also referred to as the Tribe of Dreams.

The Oneiroi emerge each night from their home in the midst of Erebus (The Darkness) where the dark mists encircle the world and fill the deep hollows of the earth.

In Hesiod's Theogony, the Oneiroi are the offspring of Nyx (The Night) with no father, whereas Hyginus and Cicero name Erebus (The Darkness) as their father.

In ancient Greece, dreams were not something that a person simply dreamed from their own mind (as in I *had* a dream), but rather, they were something external that was shown *to* them (as in I *saw* a dream, or a dream was *shown to* me).

For example, in Homer's Iliad (II, 4-22), Zeus sends an Oneiros to appear to Agamemnon, the commander of the Greek army during the Trojan War. The Oneiros takes the shape of Agamemnon's trusted advisor Nestor, and speaks to Agamemnon as Zeus instructed him, urging him into battle.

The Romans knew the Oneiroi as the Somnia (dream shapes). Ovid in his Metamorphoses goes further and names Hypnos (Sleep) as the father of the Oneiroi, and Pasithea (the personification of relaxation, meditation, and hallucinations) as their mother.

Ovid also names Morpheus (The Shaper of Dreams) as the leader of the Oneiroi. Morpheus appears in human form, Icelos or Phobetor appear as beasts, and Phantasos appears as inanimate objects.

The Oneiroi that bring truthful dreams enter the world through a gate made of horn, whereas false dreams enter the world through a gate made of ivory.

The Gates of Horn and Ivory is a literary device consisting of a play on words, where the word for horn (*κέρας*) is similar to the word fulfil (*κραίνω*), and the word for ivory (*ἐλέφας*) is similar to the word for deceive (*ἐλεφαίρομαι*).

This literary device appears in Homer's Odyssey (XIX, 560-569), and among others such as Plato's Charmides, Nonnus's Dionysiaca, and Virgil's Aeneid. However this play on words does not translate well into English.

Persephone (The Underworld and Spring Growth)

Greek Name(s): Περσεφονη, Persephonê, Persephone
Roman Name(s): Proserpina

Persephone is the Olympian goddess and queen of the underworld, and the goddess of spring growth.

She is sometimes depicted as a young goddess holding sheafs of grain and a flaming torch.

Persephone is the daughter of Zeus (the god of the sky and ruler of Olympus) and Demeter (the goddess of agriculture).

Persephone was in a flowery meadow when she was abducted by Hades and taken down to the Underworld to be his wife.

Her mother Demeter frantically searched all over the world for her, assisted by Hecate with her torches.

When Demeter finally learned that Persephone had been taken to the Underworld by Hades to be his wife, she was devastated.

When Demeter further learned that Zeus (Persephone's own father) had given Hades his approval for the abduction, Demeter was furious.

She immediately stopped her duties as the goddess of agriculture and refused to allow the earth to bear fruit until her daughter was returned. The earth turned barren, and all life on earth was at risk of starvation.

Zeus finally agreed to Demeter's demand for Persephone's return, but because Persephone had eaten a handful of pomegranate seeds from the Underworld she was then bound to the Underworld. She was forced to spend part of the year in the Underworld, and the rest of the year up on the earth.

Her yearly return to the earth is marked by the flowering of the meadows and the growth of spring. Her return to the Underworld is marked by the dying down of plants, a pause in growth, and the onset of winter.

According to the Orphic tradition, Persephone and Hades produced the Erinyes (Ερινυς, Ερινυες, Erinys, Erinyes) also known as The Furies, three goddesses of vengeance and retribution who punish people for their crimes. Their names are Tisiphone, Megaria, and Alecto.

In the Eleusinian Mysteries, Persephone's return from the Underworld is seen as a symbol of resurrection and immortality.

Phanes (The Creator)

Greek Name(s): *Φανης*, Phanês, Phanes
Roman Name(s): Protogonus

In the Orphic tradition, Phanes is the Primordial god of creation. He is the generator of life, and the driving force behind reproduction in the early cosmos.

At the dawn of creation, the Cosmic Egg or World Egg existed in the Aether (Bright Upper-Heaven). Ananke (Necessity) and Chronos (Time) in their serpent form entwined themselves around the Cosmic Egg or World Egg and caused it to break open.

Phanes hatched forth from the egg along with a chaotic mix of primordial matter, and Phanes then used the primordial matter to create the earth, the sea, and the sky.

After all creation was complete, Phanes handed over his sceptre to his daughter Nyx (The Night). Nyx then handed the sceptre to her son Uranus (The Sky). The sceptre was then seized from Uranus by Cronus (Time), and then from Cronus by Zeus, the ultimate ruler of the Cosmos. Some accounts suggest that Zeus devoured Phanes in order to absorb his power and then redistribute it among the new generation of gods known as the Olympians.

The Orphics saw Phanes as similar to the Primordial personification of desire Eros, as described in Hesiod's Theogony.

Phanes is described as a beautiful golden-winged hermaphroditic deity entwined by a serpent. His name means to bring to light or make appear from the Greek words *phanaô* and *phainô*.

Phobos (Fear)

Greek Name(s): Φοβος, Phobos, Phobos
Roman Name(s): Pavor, Terror

Phobos is a personification (daimon) of fear, translating literally as panic, specifically the panic in the midst of battle, whereas his brother Deimos personifies fear and dread before battle.

The astrological symbol for Phobos is the upper case Greek letter Phi (Φ, ph).

Hesiod's Theogony (934-936) states:

"ῥινοτόρῳ Κυθέρεια Φόβον καὶ Δεῖμον ἔτικτε δεινούς, οἵτ' ἀνδρῶν πυκινὰς κλονέουσι φάλαγγας ἐν πολέμῳ κρυόεντι σὺν Ἄρηι πτολιπόρθῳ,"

"Cytherea (Aphrodite), Fear (Phobos) and Panic (Deimos) bore, the shield-piercers
sufferers, who shake a phalanx of men thickly
in war with Ares, destroyer of towns,"

They are the sons of Ares (the god of War), who accompany their father into battle, driving his chariot and spreading fear in his wake, accompanied by Eris (the goddess of Discord). As sons of Aphrodite (the goddess of Love), they also represent the fear of loss.

In 1877 the American astronomer Asaph Hall discovered two satellites around the planet Mars, and they were appropriately named Deimos and Phobos. Deimos is the outer and the smaller of the two satellites of Mars.

In the publication Astronomische Nachrichten (Astronomy News), Volume 2, 1878, p.47 Hall writes:

"Since there is but little need of names for these satellites, I have delayed in making a selection; but in order to avoid confusion, I have chosen the following names:

*Deimus for the outer satellite.
Phobus for the inner satellite.*

These names were suggested by Mr. Madan, of Eton, England. They occur in Book XV of the Iliad, line 119, where Ares is preparing to descend to the Earth to avenge the death of his son".

The line which Hall refers to is here translated by R Lattimore:

"So he [Ares] spoke, and ordered Deimos (Fear) and Phobos (Terror) to harness his horses, and himself got into his shining armour."

Phoebe (The Shining One)

Greek Name(s): *Φοίβη*, Phoibê, Phoebe
Roman Name(s): Phoibe

Phoebe is the Titan goddess of the bright intellect and the Oracle of Delphi. She is one of the first generation of Titans born of Uranus (The Sky) and Gaia (The Earth). Her name means bright, shining, and also prophet.

She was the original goddess of the Oracle of Delphi before giving it to her grandson Apollo. Phoebe and her brother Coeus (The Enquirer) produced Leto (the goddess of childhood), and Asteria (the goddess of Delos).

Hesiod in his Theogony (404-409) writes:

φοίβη δ' αὖ Κοίου πολυήρατον ἦλθεν ἐς εὐνήν: *κυσαμένη δὴ ἔπειτα θεὰ θεοῦ ἐν φιλότητι*	Again, Phoebe came to the desired embrace of Coeus. Then the goddess through the love of the god conceived
Λητὼ κυανόπεπλον ἐγείνατο, μείλιχον αἰεί, *ἤπιον ἀνθρώποισι καὶ ἀθανάτοισι θεοῖσιν,*	and brought forth dark-gowned Leto, always mild, kind to men and to the deathless gods,
μείλιχον ἐξ ἀρχῆς, ἀγανώτατον ἐντὸς Ὀλύμπου. *γείνατο δ' Ἀστερίην ἐυώνυμον,*	mild from the beginning, gentlest in all Olympus. Also she bore Asteria of happy name

Physis (Nature and the Natural Order)

Greek Name(s): Φυσις, Phusis, Physis, Physis
Roman Name(s): Natura

In the Orphic tradition Physis is the Primordial personification of nature who emerged at the beginning of creation.

The Romans knew her as Natura (literally nature). She is also described as the *Protogeneia* (the first born) in Greek, and *Primagena* in Latin.

As well as personifying and representing nature, Physis came to represent the order of nature, and the natural order of things. According to Nonnus in his Dionysiaca, Physis (Natura) helped repair the earth after Zeus's world-shattering battle with the monster Typhoeus.

"καὶ ταμίη κόσμοιο, παλιγγενέος Φύσις ὕλης,
ῥηγνυμένης κενεῶνα κεχηνότα πῆξεν ἀρούρης,
νησαίους δὲ τένοντας ἀποτμηγέντας ἐναύλων
ἁρμονίης ἀλύτοιο πάλιν σφρηγίσσατο δεσμῷ."

"Then Physis, who governs the universe and recreates its substance, closed up the gaping rents in earth's broken surface, and sealed once more with the bond of indivisible joinery those island cliffs which had been rent from their bed."

In Seneca's Oedipus, Oedipus invokes Natura (Physis) when describing how he left home in order to avoid a prophecy that he would kill his father and marry his mother:

"non ego penates profugus excessi meos:	"Not as a fugitive did I leave my home;
parum ipse fidens mihimet in tuto tua,	of my own will, distrustful of myself,
natura, posui iura."	O Natura, I made thy laws secure"

Also in Seneca's Phaedra, the chorus invoke Nature as the mother of the gods and Zeus, to ask them why they dwell so far away, and could do more to reward the good and punish the bad:

"O magna parens, Natura, deum	"O Natura (Nature), mighty mother of the gods,
tuque igniferi rector Olympi,	and thou, fire-bearing Olympus lord
...	...
cur tanta tibi cura perennes	why dost thou dwell afar
...	...
hominum nimium securus abes,	all too indifferent to men,
non sollicitus	not anxious
prodesse bonis, nocuisse malis?"	to bring blessing to the good, and to the evil, bane?"

Polyhymnia (Muse of Sacred Poetry and Hymns)

Greek Name(s): Πολυμνια, Polymnia, Polyhymnia
Roman Name(s): Polyhymnia

Polyhymnia is the Olympian Muse of sacred poetry and religious hymns, and she is also associated with dance, eloquence, agriculture, pantomime, geometry, and meditation. She is one of the nine Muses who dwell at either Mount Helicon or Mount Parnassus, the daughters of Zeus and Mnemosyne (the goddess of Memory).

Her name can be translated as the one of many hymns (*poly-* = many + *hymnos* = hymn or praise). She is depicted in a pensive or meditative pose.

Italian poet Dante Alighieri in his Divine Comedy refers to Polyhymnia and the Muses in Paradiso, Canto 23 (55-60):

*Se mo sonasser tutte quelle lingue
che Polimnïa con le suore fero
del latte lor dolcissimo più pingue,*

If all the tongues that Polyhymnia
together with her sisters made most rich
with sweetest milk, should come now to assist

*per aiutarmi, al millesmo del vero
non si verria, cantando il santo riso
e quanto il santo aspetto facea mero;*

my singing of the holy smile that lit
the holy face of Beatrice, the truth
would not be reached—not its one-thousandth part.

Pontus (God of the Waters)

Greek Name(s): Ποντος, Pontos, Pontus
Roman Name(s): Pontus

Pontus is the Primordial personification of the sea, particularly the vast wide expanse of the sea. He is depicted as a powerful bearded man rising from the waters, or sometimes as a large floating head with a watery grey beard and crab claw horns on his head.

According to Hesiod's Theogony Pontus was born of Gaia (The Earth) without a father, but Hyginus names Aether or Uranus as his father.

After the castration of Pontus's brother Uranus, Pontus and Gaia (The Earth) together produced Nereus (the old man of the sea), Thaumas (the awe-inspiring wonder of the sea), Phorcys (a sea god associated with sea monsters), Ceto (a mighty sea goddess), and Eurybia (a goddess of the sea whose name means wide force).

These offspring of Pontus and Gaia populated the seas and oceans with various beings, from gentle nymphs to fearsome monsters.

Pontus himself did not have many myths dedicated to him, but his descendants and the sea itself had an immense significance for the ancient Greeks who were surrounded by the sea, which was both a source of sustenance and a realm of danger.

Poseidon (God of the Sea)

Greek Name(s): Ποσειδων, Poseidôn, Poseidon
Roman Name(s): Neptunus, Neptune

Poseidon is the Olympian god of the sea, earthquakes, floods, droughts, and also horses. He is depicted as an old man holding a trident (a fisherman's spear, tri = three + dent = tooth). His Roman equivalent is Neptunus or Neptune.

At birth Poseidon was swallowed whole by his father Cronus along with his siblings, but Zeus later gained the assistance of Metis who fed Cronus with a magical elixir causing Cronus to vomit back up Poseidon and his siblings.

Poseidon's trident was crafted for him with magical powers by the Cyclopes (the one-eyed giants: Brontes, Stereops, and Arges) a weapon with which he is famously associated with.

After the ten year war known as the Titanomachy and the defeat and overthrow of the Titans by the Olympians, Poseidon claimed joint rulership over the cosmos with his Olympian brothers Zeus and Hades. They drew lots to decide which of the realms they would rule. Zeus had the sky, Poseidon had the sea, and Hades had the Underworld.

Poseidon seduced many nymphs and mortal woman often in the guise of an animal or flowing water. Some of his most famous conquests were the Gorgon Medusa, Tyro, Amymone, and Aithra mother of the hero Theseus. In one myth Poseidon entered a contest with the goddess Athena for dominion over Athens and produced the very first horse as a gift. But the king refused him the prize and in anger Poseidon afflicted the land with drought.

The Homeric Hymn to Poseidon reads:

*"ἀμφὶ Ποσειδάωτα, μέγαν θεόν, ἄρχομ' ἀείδειν,
γαίης κινητῆρα καὶ ἀτρυγέτοιο θαλάσσης,*

*πόντιον, ὅσθ' Ἑλικῶνα καὶ εὐρείας ἔχει Αἰγάς.
διχθά τοι, Ἐννοσίγαιε, θεοὶ τιμὴν ἐδάσαντο,*

ἵππων τε δμητῆρ' ἔμεναι σωτῆρά τε νηῶν.

χαῖρε, Ποσείδαον γαιήοχε, κυανοχαῖτα,

καί, μάκαρ, εὐμενὲς ἦτορ ἔχων πλώουσιν ἄρηγε."

"I begin to sing about Poseidon,

the great god, mover of the earth and fruitless sea,
god of the deep who is also lord of Helicon and wide Aegae.
A two-fold office the gods allotted you, O Shaker of the Earth,
to be a tamer of horses and a saviour of ships!
Hail, Poseidon, Holder of the Earth, dark-haired lord!
O blessed one, be kindly in heart and help those who voyage in ships!"

Prometheus (Forethought and Fire)

Greek Name(s): *Προμηθευς*, Promêtheus, Prometheus
Roman Name(s): Prometheus

Prometheus is the Titan god of forethought, fire, and wise counsel. His brother is Epithemeus whose name means afterthought.

Some sources name their parents as Iapetus and Asia or Clymene.

Prometheus is known for having stolen fire from the Olympian gods and giving fire to humanity in the form of technology, knowledge, and more generally, civilisation. For this he was punished by Zeus who condemned him to eternal torment.

Prometheus was bound to a rock, and an eagle was sent to eat his liver (which the ancient Greeks believed was the centre of human emotions).

During the night his liver would grow back, only to be eaten by the eagle again the next day.

Prometheus is also known for creating humanity from clay, and for his intelligence, and being a champion of humankind.

Prometheus became a figure who represented the human striving for greater knowledge and for technical and scientific advancement to improve the quality of life for humankind, and also the idea of overreaching and the unintended consequences of such endeavours.

Aeschylus writes in Prometheus Bound that he gave humanity the spiritess (daimona) Elpis (Hope) or the spiritesses (daimones) Elpides (The Hopes) in order help them to ignore Moros.

Προμηθεύς
θνητούς γ' ἔπαυσα μὴ προδέρκεσθαι μόρον.

Prometheus
Yes, I caused mortals to cease foreseeing their doom.

Χορός
τὸ ποῖον εὑρὼν τῆσδε φάρμακον νόσου;

Chorus
Of what sort was the cure that you found for this affliction?

Προμηθεύς
τυφλὰς ἐν αὐτοῖς ἐλπίδας κατῴκισα.

Prometheus
I caused blind hopes to dwell within their breasts.

Χορός
μέγ' ὠφέλημα τοῦτ' ἐδωρήσω βροτοῖς.

Chorus
A great benefit was this you gave to mortals.

Rhea (Queen of the Heavens)

Greek Name(s): *Ρεια*, *Ρεα*, Rheia, Rhea
Roman Name(s): Magna Mater, Ops, Opis

Rhea is a Titan mother goddess, queen of the the heavens, and the mother of the eldest Olympian gods (Hestia, Demeter, Hera, Poseidon, Hades, and Zeus). Her name means flow or ease, and as such she represents the eternal flow of time and generations, and comfort and ease. The Romans knew her as Ops, and also Magna Mater (great mother) sometimes identifying her with the mother goddess Cybele. Like the mother goddess Cybele, she is often depicted with lions.

As the mother of the gods, Rhea symbolises and represents motherhood and fertility. She is the daughter of Uranus (The Sky) and Gaia (The Earth), and the wife of Cronus (Time).

Rhea's brother and husband Cronus feared being overthrown by his offspring, and so he swallowed each of their children as they were born. When Rhea bore the sixth and final child Zeus, she had him spirited him away to Crete under the protection of the nymph Amalthea to be raised in hiding.

Rhea appointed three, five, or nine rustic spirits (daimones) called the Curetes (*Κουρητη*, *Κουρητες*, Kourêtê, Kourêtes) or the Dactyli (*Δακτυλος*, *Δακτυλοι*, Daktylos, Daktyloi) to guard Zeus in a cave on Mount Ida. They drowned out the infant cries of Zeus with dancing and clashing their shields with spears.

Rhea then tricked Cronus into swallowing a rock wrapped in swaddling bands instead, believing it to be Zeus. Zeus was assisted by Metis who gave Cronus an emetic, making him vomit back up the children he had swallowed. Zeus eventually overthrew his father Cronus and the Titans.

Selene (The Moon)

Greek Name(s): Σεληνη, Selênê, Selene
Roman Name(s): Luna

Selene is the Titan goddess of the moon. She is the daughter of Hyperion and Theia, and the sister of Helios (The Sun), and Eos (The Dawn). Her name comes from the ancient Greek selas (σέλας) meaning light, brightness, or gleam. She drives her moon chariot across the heavens each night.

She is also called Mene, and the Phrygian peoples of Anatolia and the surrounding areas called her Men. The Stoic philosopher Chrysippus interpreted the two names Selene and Men as female and male aspects of the same god.

Selene is often depicted with a crescent moon, a chariot, a torch, and a billowing cloak. The Romans knew her as Luna, and her day of the week is Monday, which the Romans called Lunae Dies (moon day).

She is frequently associated and identified with Artemis (Diana) and Hecate who are also considered to be strongly associated with the moon.

Selene is sometimes associated with childbirth, due to the belief that during the full moon women had the easiest of labours giving birth, this was instrumental in her being identified with Artemis (Diana).

In the Orphic tradition The Moirai (Three Fates) were identified as three divisions of Selene, the crescent moon, the full moon, and the dark moon, and thus the phases of the moon represented the turning of the wheel of time, and the wheel of fate.

Tartarus (The Darkest Depths)

Greek Name(s): *Ταρταρος*, Tartaros, Tartarus
Roman Name(s): Tartarus

Tartarus is the Primordial elemental deity of the great pit that lies beneath the Earth (Gaia), and at the bottom of the Underworld (Hades). According to Hesiod's Theogony, Tartarus is the third to emerge at the dawn of creation after Chaos and Gaia. Hesiod also says that a bronze anvil falling from the heavens would fall for nine days before it reached the earth, and would then take a further nine days to fall from the earth down to Tartarus.

The cosmos is imagined as a great sphere where the dome of the sky is at the top, the flat disc of the earth is in the middle, and Hades and the pit of Tartarus is at the bottom.

After the Titans were overthrown by Zeus, Coeus and his brothers (except Oceanus) were imprisoned in Tartarus, secured by a wall of bronze with gates guarded by the hundred-handed Hekatoncheires. Later Coeus was overcome with madness, broke free from his bonds, and attempted to escape from his imprisonment, but he was repelled by Cerberus, the multi-headed Hound of Hades (Hesiod suggests fifty heads, others suggest three). According to Pindar and Aeschylus, the Titans were eventually released from Tartarus because of Zeus's clemency.

Tartarus was later imagined as not only the prison of the Titans, but as place of judgement of souls, and a dungeon of torment for the wicked to receive divine punishment.

Tartarus and Gaia together produced Typhoeus, a monstrous serpentine storm giant. Zeus defeated the creature and cast it back down to the pit of Tartarus, and from there it remained as the cosmic source of hurricanes and storm winds.

Terpsichore (Muse of Dance)

Greek Name(s): *Τερψιχορη*, Terpsikhorê, Terpsichore
Roman Name(s): Terpsichore

Terpsichore is the Olympian Muse of dance and the chorus, and one of the nine Muses who dwell at either Mount Helicon or Mount Parnassus, the daughters of Zeus and Mnemosyne (the goddess of Memory).

Her name means delighting in dance from the Greek words *terpsis* to delight and *khoros* dance, the origin of the English words terpsichoreal and terpsichorean, meaning of or relating to dance. Terpsichore is often depicted in a seated position holding a lyre, accompanying dancers and choirs with her music.

From the 1st century BCE to the 3rd century CE the demand for Roman copies of Greek statues throughout the Roman Empire had increased dramatically. Emperor Hadrian's villa in modern day Tivoli, Italy, had a 1.5 metre marble statue of Terpsichore which is now at the Prado Museum in Madrid.

The Great Gymnasium of Pompeii is home to the Moregine frescoes. In the first triclinium are a series of frescoes depicting the Muses, including Terpsichore. In 1739 the French painter Jean-Marc Nattier completed his painting of Terpsichore which is now in the Fine Arts Museums of San Francisco.

According to Apollonius of Rhodes, Terpsichore was the mother of three Sirens by the river god Achelous named Thelxinoe or Thelxiope, Aglaphonus, and Molpe. There are however multiple sources naming seven different parentages (including Terpsichore's sisters Melpomene or Calliope), and fifteen different Siren names.

Tethys (The Earth-Nourishing Waters)

Greek Name(s): *Τηθυς*, Têthys, Tethys
Roman Name(s): Tethys

Tethys is the Titan goddess of the earth-nourishing waters, the sister and wife of Oceanus (The Earth River), and the mother of the three thousand Potamoi (River Gods), the three thousand Oceanids (water nymphs), and the Nephelai (rain clouds). Tethys is the daughter of Uranus (The Sky) and Gaia (The Earth).

Her name was derived from the Greek word *têthê* meaning nurse or grandmother. The Roman poet Claudian wrote that Tethys nursed Helios and Selene, the offspring of her siblings Hyperion and Theia, until they came of age and achieved their full luminosity.

Tethys plays a small part in Greek mythology with no known established cults of worship, making her something of a peripheral figure. She does appear frequently in paintings on Greek vases accompanied by Eileithyia (the goddess of childbirth), and her husband Oceanus (The Waters).

Tethys also appears in mosaic art next to Oceanus with a small pair of wings on top of her head, possibly signifying her role as the mother of rain clouds. The name Tethys became increasingly used in a poetic sense to refer to the sea, and as such, the identity and iconography of Tethys had begun to merge with that of the sea goddess Thalassa into one.

The Tethys Sea also refers to an ancient pre-historic sea that existed during the Mesozoic period 252 to 66 million years ago. Over time it evolved into the Indian Ocean, the Mediterranean Sea, the Black Sea, and the Caspian Sea.

Thalassa (The Primordial Sea)

Greek Name(s): Θαλασσα, Thalassa, Thalatta
Roman Name(s): Mare

Thalassa is the Primordial personification of the sea. According to Hyginus, she is the offspring of Aether (The Bright Upper-Heaven) and Hemera (The Day). As the daughter of Aether, she is therefore the sister of Gaia (The Earth) and Uranus (The Sky).

Thalassa and Pontus (The Sea) together produced the fish and other sea creatures. As amorphous elemental deities representing the sea, Thalassa and Pontus were later ruled over by the anthropomorphic Olympian gods Poseidon and Amphitrite.

The name Thalassa became increasingly used in a poetic sense to refer to the sea, and as such, the identity and iconography of Thalassa had begun to merge with that of the sea goddess Tethys into one.

Several of Aesop's fables involve Thalassa as the personification of the sea. Fable no. 276 reads:

"A farmer saw a ship and her crew about to sink into the sea as the ship's prow disappeared beneath the curl of a wave. The farmer said, O sea, it would have been better if no one had ever set sail on you! You are a pitiless element of nature and an enemy to mankind. When she heard this, Thalassa (the Sea) took on the shape of a woman and said in reply, Do not spread such evil stories about me! I am not the cause of any of these things that happen to you; the Winds (Anemoi) to which I am exposed are the cause of them all. If you look at me when the Winds are gone, and sail upon me then, you will admit that I am even more gentle than that dry land of yours."

Thalia (Muse of Comedy)

Greek Name(s): Θαλεια, Thaleia, Thalia
Roman Name(s): Thalia

Thalia (sometimes Thaleia) is the Olympian Muse of comedy, and one of the nine Muses who dwell at either Mount Helicon or Mount Parnassus, the daughters of Zeus and Mnemosyne (the goddess of Memory).

Her name means the joyous, the flourishing, from the ancient Greek θάλλειν *thállein*, to flourish, to be verdant. The latter meaning is in reference to her attribute as a muse of bucolic poetry, expressing the pleasant aspects of the countryside and country life.

She is depicted as a young woman with a joyous air, crowned with ivy, wearing boots, and holding a comic mask in her hand. Some of her statues hold a bugle, a trumpet, a shepherd's staff, or a wreath of ivy.

According to Apollodorus, Thalia and Apollo produced the Corybantes, the armed and crested dancers who worshipped the Phrygian goddess Cybele with drumming and dancing.

The Corybantes were tasked with guarding the young Zeus while he was in hiding to protect him from being devoured by Cronus. Cronus turned them into lions, and Zeus made them into kings of the animals, and Rhea yoked them to her chariot.

Thanatos (Peaceful Death)

Greek Name(s): Θανατος, Thanatos, Thanatos
Roman Name(s): Mors, Letum, Thanatus

Thanatos is the Primordial personification of death. He is often referred to but rarely appearing in person. His Roman equivalent is Mors or Letum. According to Hesiod's Theogony, Thanatos is the son of Nyx without a father. Hyginus and Cicero both name Erebus as the father.

Next to his twin brother Hypnos (Sleep), Thanatos lives in a cave in the Underworld (Hades) where the river Lethe (Forgetfulness) comes from, where day and night meet, but where no sunlight or sound enters. At the entrance to his cave there are poppies growing, along with other sleep inducing plants.

Hypnos and Thanatos are the subject of a painting by John William Waterhouse called Sleep and His Half-Brother Death, depicting the two figures side by side. The lighter figure in the foreground is Sleep (Hypnos) holding poppies in his hands, and the darker figure in the background is Death (Thanatos).

Hypnos, and other descendents of Nyx such as Thanatos and Morpheus, have long been metaphorically associated with trance, sleep, and death, and in art they have long been depicted with poppies, scattering poppies, or with poppies nearby.

"ἔνθα δὲ Νυκτὸς παῖδες ἐρεμνῆς οἰκί' ἔχουσιν,
Ὕπνος καὶ Θάνατος, δεινοὶ θεοί: οὐδέ ποτ' αὐτοὺς
Ἥλιος φαέθων ἐπιδέρκεται ἀκτίνεσσιν

οὐρανὸν εἰς ἀνιὼν οὐδ' οὐρανόθεν καταβαίνων.
τῶν δ' ἕτερος γαῖάν τε καὶ εὐρέα νῶτα θαλάσσης
ἥσυχος ἀνστρέφεται καὶ μείλιχος ἀνθρώποισι,

τοῦ δὲ σιδηρέη μὲν κραδίη, χάλκεον δέ οἱ ἦτορ
νηλεὲς ἐν στήθεσσιν: ἔχει δ' ὃν πρῶτα λάβῃσιν
ἀνθρώπων: ἐχθρὸς δὲ καὶ ἀθανάτοισι θεοῖσιν."

"but the other holds in her arms Sleep the brother of Death,
even evil Night, wrapped in a vaporous cloud.
And there the children of dark Night have their dwellings, Sleep and Death, awful gods.
The glowing Sun never looks upon them with his beams,
neither as he goes up into heaven, nor as he comes down from heaven.
And the former of them roams peacefully over the earth and the sea's broad back and is kindly to men;
but the other has a heart of iron, and his spirit within him
is pitiless as bronze: whomever of men he has once seized he holds fast:
and he is hateful even to the deathless gods."

Theia (The Wide-Shining One)

Greek Name(s): Θεια, Theia, Aithre
Roman Name(s): Theia

Theia is the Titan goddess of sight, brilliance, and the shining ether of the bright blue sky.

She is the goddess who gives gold, silver, and gems with their brilliance. Her name comes from the Greek words *thea* sight and *theiazô* prophesy. She is also named Aithre blue sky, and Euryphaessa wide-shining.

Theia features only slightly in Greek mythology, but she is an important figure because of her descendants.

According to Hesiod's Theogony, Theia was born of Uranus (The Sky) and Gaia (The Earth). Theia and her brother Hyperion produced Helios (The Sun), Selene (The Moon), and Eos (The Dawn).

The Roman poet Catullus in his Carmina (no. 66) described Helios, Selene, and Eos as the three lights of the heavens and Theia's illustrious progeny.

The Greek poet Pindar praised Theia in his fifth Isthmian ode:

> "μᾶτερ Ἀλίου πολυώνυμε Θεία,
> σέο ἕκατι καὶ μεγασθενῆ νόμισαν
> χρυσὸν ἄνθρωποι περιώσιον ἄλλων:"

> "Mother of the Sun, Theia of many names,
> for your sake men honor as more powerful
> gold than anything else;"

Themis (Divine Order, Justice, and Custom)

Greek Name(s): Θεμις, Themis, Themis
Roman Name(s): Justitia

Themis is the Titan goddess of justice, divine law, divine order, and custom. She is one of the twelve Titan children of Gaia (The Earth) and Uranus (The Sky).

She is the second wife of Zeus, and is associated with oracles and prophecies, including the Oracle of Delphi. Her symbol is the scales of justice. She is also associated with the Roman goddess Justitia, literally justice.

She is often depicted as a serious looking woman holding scales of justice, and sometimes a sword. When she is disregarded, the goddess Nemesis punishes those who have disregarded her. She shared a temple with Nemesis at Rhamnous.

Judges were often referred to as *themistopóloi* (the many [servants] of Themis), and so it was for the maintenance of divine order on Mount Olympus. Hera, queen of the gods, addressed her politely and respectfully as Lady Themis.

Themis received the Oracle at Delphi from Gaia, and then gave it to Phoebe, who then gave it to her grandson Apollo. Themis was present at Delos to witness the birth of Apollo, and nursed him with ambrosia (the food of the gods) and nectar.

Hyginus in his De Astronomica lists Themis alongside the nymph Amalthea as the foster-mother and nurse of the young Zeus.

Thesis (Creation)

Greek Name(s): *Θεσις, Θετις*, Thesis, Thetis
Roman Name(s): Thesis

According to the Orphic tradition, Thesis is the female Primordial personification of creation, cosmic harmony, and balance.

Thesis emerged at the beginning of creation before the existence of even time itself. There are several varying accounts regarding the sequence of events and the emergence of the Primordial deities.

Thesis is sometimes portrayed as the female aspect of Phanes (The Creator), and sometimes Thesis is described as the divine mother or grandmother of Phanes.

According to Orphic Fragments 54 and 57, Thesis and Hydros (The Primordial Waters) together produced Chronos (Time) and Ananke (Necessity), who entwined themselves around the Cosmic-Egg or World-Egg.

Phanes hatched forth from the egg along with a chaotic mix of primordial matter, which he then used to create the earth, the sea, and the sky.

While Thesis does not feature as prominently in Greek mythology as other deities, she was venerated in the Orphic mystery cults, which held her in high regard for her role in the creation of the cosmos.

Triton (God of the Depths of the Sea)

Greek Name(s): *Τριτων*, *Tritôn*, Triton
Roman Name(s): Triton

Triton is an Olympian god of the sea, and the son of Poseidon and Amphitrite.

He is the ruler or the possessor of the depths of the sea, and he lives with his parents in a golden palace on the sea bed.

Triton is depicted as a merman with a human-like upper-body, and the lower body of a fish (sometimes with a single fish tail, and from the late 2nd century BCE onwards a double fish tail).

In mosaic art he is also depicted with crab claw horns, green tinged skin, and from the 2nd century BCE onwards with the forelegs of a horse, a creature also known as an *ichthyocentaur*.

Ovid describes his shoulders as being barnacled with sea-shells.

Sometimes carrying a trident like his father Poseidon, Triton also had conch-shell which he blew like a trumpet in order to calm or rouse the waves.

Pseudo-Hyginus said that the sound of Triton's conch-shell trumpet was so cacophonous that when it was blown loudly, the giants scattered believing it to be the sound of a giant beast.

In later literature Triton is portrayed as the messenger or the herald of Poseidon and Oceanus. Triton(s) became a generic term for a merman (mermen) in art and literature.

In the art of the 4th century BCE, Triton was sometimes multiplied into a large group of spirits (daimones) called Tritones.

Triton was also described as the god of the Tritonis, a large salt lake in Libya. When the Argonauts found themselves stranded in the middle of the desert, he helped them find passage from the lake back to the sea.

From around the 3rd century BCE the Sirens of Homer's Odyssey were sometimes depicted on pottery as Tritons rather than the traditional human-headed birds (e.g. the mold-made Megarian bowl from Cistern on Areopagus, from the excavation of the Athenian Agora, catalogued P 18,640). This marks the beginning of the cultural and iconographic overlap between mermen, mermaids, and sirens.

Triton appeared in Roman literature in Virgil's Aeneid, and the poet Valerius Flaccus, who wrote in his Argonautica that there were two Tritons, one on each side of Neptune's chariot, holding the reins of the horses.

Tyche (Goddess of Fortune and Luck)

Greek Name(s): *Τυχη*, Tykhê, Tyche, Tyche
Roman Name(s): Fortuna

Tyche is the Titan goddess of fortune, chance, providence, and fate. Her Roman equivalent is Fortuna (fortune).

She is the daughter of Oceanus (The Waters) and Tethys (The Waters), and therefore one of the Oceanids.

As well as personal fate, Tyche presides over the fate of communities, towns, and cities.

Sometimes she is named as a daughter of Zeus in other sources, and described as bringing positive messages to people relating to external events outside their control.

She is often depicted with a rudder or a ship's wheel, symbolising her influence on the course of events, literally steering a course. The ship's wheel is also the wheel of fortune representing the cyclical nature of fortune and misfortune.

In the time of Alexander the Great, the positive and negative whims of fate were embodied as much by Tyche as the Twelve Olympians. The Greek historian Polybius believed that when no cause could be discovered for events such as floods, droughts, or frosts, then the cause may be attributed to Tyche.

She is associated with the goddess Nemesis, who restores a sense of balance by bringing loss upon those who have been favoured too generously by Tyche. They became increasingly worshipped side by side, sharing cult status either as two equal opposite deities, or with one being an aspect of the other.

Resurgences of the worship of Tyche often occurred during times of instability and uncertain change, where those fearful of the future would pray for her to deliver them through difficult times. By contrast, poets of the ages would lament and bemoan her sudden and unaccountable changes of mood or behaviour.

Her Roman equivalent Fortuna is addressed in the anonymous goliardic poem O Fortuna written around the 13th century in the monastery of Benediktbeuern, in southern Germany.

"O Fortuna velut luna statu variabilis,

semper crescis aut decrescis; vita detestabilis
nunc obdurat et tunc curat ludo mentis aciem,
egestatem, potestatem dissolvit ut glaciem."

"O Fortune, like the moon you are changeable,
ever waxing ever waning; hateful life

first oppresses and then soothes playing with mental clarity;
poverty and power it melts them like ice."

Urania (Muse of Astronomy)

Greek Name(s): *Oυρανιη*, Ouraniê, Urania
Roman Name(s): Urania

Urania is the Olympian Muse of astronomy and the stars, and one of the nine Muses who dwell at either Mount Helicon or Mount Parnassus, the daughters of Zeus and Mnemosyne (the goddess of Memory). Her name means heavenly or of heaven, and is sometimes used as an epithet to other gods such as Aphrodite Urania (heavenly Aphrodite).

Urania is able to foretell the future by interpreting the arrangement of the stars, and is often depicted holding a compass, a small staff, and a globe representing a celestial sphere. She wears a cloak embroidered with the stars.

According to Diodorus Siculus, those who are most concerned with philosophy and the heavens are dearest to her, and those who have been instructed by her are raised aloft to heaven by her. She is also associated with universal love who inherited the majesty and power of her father Zeus, and the grace of her mother Mnemosyne.

Some sources suggest that Urania is the mother of Linus, a mythical legendary musician and master of eloquent speech, with Apollo, Hermes, or Poseidon's son Amphimarus as the father.

Urania is also named as the mother of Hymenaios (Roman: Talasius), the god of weddings and the wedding hymn called the hymenaios, a traditional genre of Greek poetry that was sung during the procession of the bride to the groom's house in which the god is addressed. Other sources name Clio, Calliope, or Terpsichore as his mother.

Uranus (God of the Sky)

Greek Name(s): *Ουρανος*, Ouranos, Uranus
Roman Name(s): Caelus

Uranus is the Primordial personification of the sky, imagined as a solid dome whose edges descend to rest upon the outermost limits of the disc-shaped earth. His Roman equivalent is Caelus (the heavens).

According to Hesiod, Uranus was created by Gaia (The Earth) to "cover her on every side", and to provide an "abiding place for the blessed gods".

The Orphic tradition suggests that Uranus was born of the Cosmic-Egg or World-Egg, or fashioned out of the contents of the world egg by the creator god Phanes.

Uranus and Gaia had twelve sons and six daughters. Three of his sons were the one-eyed giants known as the Cyclopes (Brontes, Stereops, and Arges).

Another three were the giants known as the Hecatoncheires, the hundred-handed ones (Cottus, Briareus, and Gyges) who Uranus hid deep inside Gaia (The Earth).

Next came the Titans (Iapetus, Cronus, Rhea, Hyperion, Coeus, Phoebe, Themis, Mnemosyne, Oceanus, Tethys, and Crius). Uranus hated all of his offspring, and the feeling was mutual.

Uranus's sons conspired against their father Uranus, laying an ambush for him as he descended to Gaia in order to lay with her. They waited at the four corners of the world and seized hold of Uranus, and held him down while Cronus, who waited in the centre, castrated Uranus with the stone sickle that Gaia had made especially, and then threw his severed genitals into the sea.

According to Hesiod, after Uranus's genitals were thrown into the sea, a foam spread, out of which the goddess Aphrodite emerged (*ἀφρός*, aphrós = foam). This contrasts with Homer's account that Aphrodite was the daughter of Zeus and Dione.

Uranus's blood splattered onto the earth which produced the Erinyes (The Furies), the Gigantes (The Giants), and the Meliae (Ash-Tree Nymphs). Uranus was furious at his offspring, and named them the Titans, meaning the strained ones, saying that vengeance for the deed would follow. Uranus retreated to the background after this event, becoming simply the sky, rotated on an axis by Atlas.

The ancient Greeks and Romans knew of only five wandering stars (*πλανῆται*, planetai = planets) which were given the Roman names for the gods: Mercury (Hermes), Venus (Aphrodite), Mars (Ares), Jupiter (Zeus), and Saturn (Cronus). When a sixth planet was discovered in 1781 using a telescope, it took until the mid-19th century for the name Uranus to be agreed upon, which unlike the other planets is based on the Greek name rather than the Roman name.

Zeus (King of the Gods)

Greek Name(s): Ζευς, Zeus, Zeus
Roman Name(s): Jupiter, Jove

Zeus is the King of the Gods, the ruler of the skies, the weather, law and order, destiny, fate, and kingship. He is also called the sky father.

His Roman equivalent is Jupiter or Jove, and he decides the roles of the other gods who treat him with reverence and respect.

He is often depicted with a royal sceptre, an eagle (a sign of immortality), and holding a lightning bolt which was fashioned for him as a weapon by the Cyclopes.

He was the youngest child of Cronus (Time) and Rhea (Queen of the Heavens). Cronus, having overthrown his own father Uranus, feared being overthrown by his offspring, and took to devouring them as soon as they were born.

When Rhea bore her sixth child Zeus, under the advice of her parents Uranus and Gaia, she had the infant Zeus spirited away by the nymph Amalthea to the island of Crete, and Cronus was tricked into swallowing a stone wrapped in swaddling bands believing it to be Zeus.

Zeus's mother appointed three, five, or nine rustic spirits (daimones) called the Curetes (*Κουρητη, Κουρητες*, Kourêtê, Kourêtes) or the Dactyli (*Δακτυλος, Δακτυλοι*, Daktylos, Daktyloi) to guard Zeus in a cave on Mount Ida. They drowned out his infant cries with their dancing and the clashing of their shields and spears.

When Zeus reached manhood, he was assisted by Metis in rescuing his siblings. Metis gave Cronus an emetic, making Cronus vomit back up all of the infant gods he had devoured (and the stone).

Zeus together with his siblings eventually defeated and overthrew their father Cronus and the Titans during the Titanomachy (the ten year war between the Olympians and the Titans for the control of the cosmos).

Zeus banished the Titans to Tartarus beneath the earth and at the bottom of Hades, and then became the ruler of the new generation of Olympian gods, and the supreme ruler of the cosmos.

Zeus is also well known for fathering many divine and heroic offspring within and outside of his marriages, including Agdistis, Aigipan, Aletheia, Aphrodite, Apollo, Ares, Artemis, Asopos, Ate, Athena, Britomartis, The Cabeiroi, Caerus, The Charites, Dionysus, Eileithyia, Eris, Ersa, Harmonia, Hebe, Hephaestus, Hermes, The Horai, The Litai, Melinoe, The Moirai, The Muses, Nemea, The Nymphai, The Palikoi, Pan, Pandeia, Persephone, Phasis, and Zagreus.

www.ingramcontent.com/pod-product-compliance
Lightning Source LLC
Chambersburg PA
CBHW051419070526
44584CB00023B/3504